Seven Days With Mary

by
Michael H. Brown

Published by
Faith Publishing Company
P.O. Box 237
Milford OH 45150-0237
U.S.A.

Published by: Faith Publishing Company
                          P.O. Box 237
                          Milford, Ohio 45150-0237
                          United States of America

Additional copies of this book may be acquired by contacting:

For bookstores: Faith Publishing Company
                          P.O. Box 237
                          Milford, Ohio 45150-0237
                          USA
                          Phone: 1-513-576-6400
                          Fax: 1-513-576-0022

For individuals: The Riehle Foundation
                          P.O. Box 7
                          Milford, Ohio 45150-0007
                          USA
                          Phone: 1-513-576-0032
                          Fax: 1-513-576-0022

Front cover illustration: **Christian Wilhelmy**
Photographs used with permission of Joan Carroll Cruz.

Dedication

For Maureen, my twin sister

My thanks to all who have supported me all these years in the study of the Virgin Mary, especially the Marian groups throughout the U.S. and Canada. I would like to thank my wife as always for her support, as well as Faith Publishing and in particular Bonnie Lewis and Carolyn Barnes, whose sure hands as editors always improve a book. I would also like to thank the Marian Library at the University of Dayton for its assistance and Bishop Howard Hubbard of Albany for informally reviewing the manuscript and offering helpful comments.

Preface

The Virgin Mother of God has been appearing since the first century and her appearances are so numerous that no scholar and no organization—not even our august Church—can estimate how many times she has been connected with miracles.

For twenty centuries the Blessed Mother of Nazareth has interceded on behalf of her Son. Anyone who sincerely studies her apparitions will be stunned by the number and effect of her appearances. Mary founded hundreds of the early churches, and she deeply affected major historical figures—men who shaped the very boundaries of our world—like Charlemagne.

She is the great antidote to paganism. She takes territory back from the "gods" and brings it to the One True Creator.

She is a messenger of the Trinity.

Her miracles in relatively unrecognized nations like Austria are too many to count, let alone the times she has appeared in countries like Spain, France, and Italy. The number is estimated in the thousands or tens of thousands, and many hundreds of those appearances have been sanctioned by the Church, which has built many monuments, shrines, and churches at the sites of her apparitions. Even in the relatively young nation of America she has left an indelible presence and was involved with the very founding of the New World. Christopher Columbus was extremely dedicated to the Virgin Mary (we remember his ship, the *Santa Maria*), and when French explorers arrived they originally named our greatest river the "River of the Immaculate Conception" (since known as the Mississippi).

Most recently the Virgin has been involved in the dismantling of Communism. According to Sister Lucia dos Santos, the sole surviving seer from Fatima, the triumph of Mary's Immaculate Heart as forecast at Fatima began with the fall of Communism in Eastern bloc countries. Although Communism may one day again rear its head, it is truly a miracle how, after consecration by the great John Paul II, Mary, with prayers from the faithful, brought freedom first to Poland and then to the rest of Eastern Europe and even (at least for the last few years) the Soviet Union!

Soon after Communism collapsed in Poland, Lech Walesa, the Polish freedom fighter, was photographed in front of a Fatima statue, which seemed joyful in the background.

These are just a couple examples of how Mary has interceded through the centuries. There are many other cases. We don't hear of them because the secular educators do not tell us about them. They ignore Mary and her great powers of intercession.

But intercede she does, and often. She is given certain reservoirs of grace by Jesus, and she dispenses them with exquisite generosity—constantly seeking help for us at the Throne of God.

She is the handmaid of the Lord. She is the spouse of the Holy Spirit. And we need to seek the comfort of her mantle as the world grows increasingly evil. We live in an unusual and special time. There has always been materialism, there has always been greed, there has always been immorality, but the level to which our very institutions have fallen gives great pause and recalls corrupt times like those back during the fall of

Rome or during the high Middle Ages.

We are in danger. Our families are in danger. But there is a remedy and that remedy is found in Mary. She is with us. She is here to protect us. She helps us grow closer to the Holy Spirit. While it is crucial to pray directly to Christ, and while our main prayer should always be to Jesus and the Holy Spirit (Who comes with such power, especially during Mass), the prayers of Mary have been given a special power against the particular evil of our times and are there for the asking. She prays for us. She helps us seek the consolation and guidance of her Son.

That's what this book is about: seeking the aid of Mary. Meditating on her role. Walking with her as we try to find our way through the current darkness. It is arranged so that there is a meditation each day of the week and a series of prayers focusing upon a different historical apparition. There are seven apparitions, and each should be read on a different day of the week. It doesn't matter what day you start, but it is probably best if it is done for seven consecutive days. Each day has prayers related to the apparition and the suggestion to recite the Rosary, meditating on the lessons of that day's particular apparition and invoking her through litanies and novenas. If possible, recitation of the Scriptural Rosary at the end of each session would be great.

The goal is not a history lesson. The goal is not a book about apparitions. The goal is a book of meditation and prayer that takes many of the things suggested by Heaven during the past twenty centuries and puts them into practice. For Mary's role has not been a political one. Her role is not on the world stage. Her role is spiritual preparation of her children and getting us to Heaven. Her goal is your soul. You are crucial to Heaven. You are important to the Virgin Mary. And she has come not to make big headlines but rather to help you with the intricate and difficult aspects of living upon this earth. She wants to have a personal relationship with you. She wants you to have a more personal relationship with Jesus. And that's why she comes. That's why she appears with such frequency. She has something to give everyone personally.

She has something for you.

And I pray you receive it through this book.

Meditate on each major appearance that is reviewed in this book and apply the lessons to your own lives.

There are hidden meanings.

There are hidden lessons.

In many cases, obscure and yet fascinating details about Mary's apparitions have been lost to history.

The goal here is to resurrect them.

This is a book of how to apply all that we have heard about Mary to our own personal lives. The goal is to use the current period of grace to love all fellow humans and achieve Heaven.

Every apparition used in this book has been formally approved by the Roman Catholic Church. They are officially recognized and sanctioned. At the end is a meditation and ejaculation that I devised, as well as a very brief litany related to the apparitions. They are followed by novena prayers and litanies that have been given various imprimaturs in the past and come from many different and often ancient sources.

They are *important* sources. They are relevant sources. As the world changes around us, and the landscape shifts, as we hear strange news and see strange weather, as we step with trepidation to a new era, we need the Virgin to show us the way to the Holy Spirit.

We probably have enough news of current-day apparitions. We are saturated with reputed prophets. We should never despise what they say, but we must test their words and we must have a foundation in authentic Marian devotion before heading for unchartered waters.

That foundation is in Mary's past appearances.

Enjoy studying one a day for a week. Enjoy the grace. Enjoy the feeling of peace. There are many hidden clues in Mary's miracles, and it is time to apply them with more vigor.

It is time to make sure we're fully under her mantle. It's time to make sure we are in constant touch with her spouse, the Holy Spirit.

Come Holy Spirit! Come Spirit of God and guide us on this little journey! Come Holy Spirit and teach us how best to pray! Come Holy Spirit and lift any blindness! Come Holy Spirit and bring us to the way God wants us to live our lives so that one day we may see Your Face and be worthy of Your Presence! Amen.

OUR LADY OF SARAGOSSA

OUR LADY OF MONTSERRAT

OUR LADY OF GOOD COUNSEL

OUR LADY OF GUADALUPE – SPAIN

OUR LADY OF GUADALUPE – MEXICO

OUR LADY OF THE MIRACULOUS MEDAL

OUR LADY OF LOURDES

OUR LADY OF PROMPT SUCCOR

TABLE OF CONTENTS

PAGE

First Day

Our Lady of Saragossa

And so it is that we arrive at the very first recorded miracle of the Virgin Mary, her legendary appearance in north central Spain at a place known as Saragossa (also spelled Zaragoza).

To understand this apparition, we must recall that it occurred around A.D. 40, just a few years after the death and Resurrection of Our Lord Jesus.

Some people believe that at the time of the Saragossa miracle, Mary was living with the apostle John in Jerusalem or the city of Ephesus. They say this because, at the Crucifixion, Jesus, peering down at John and Mary, had said, "Woman, there is your son," and to John, "There is your mother" (*John* 19:26-27).

According to Scripture, from that time on John took the Blessed Virgin Mary into his care.

We can only wonder at how it would have been to live with this sacred woman. To be in her presence must have been to be in a state of peace and well-being, listening to her unprecedented wisdom, feeling the strength of her ceaseless prayers. Some people claim that since St. John may have spent time in the city of Ephesus (near what is now called Kusadasi in modern-day Turkey), the Virgin Mary may also have lived there. If so, this simple and humble handmaid was in the midst of pagan territory. For at the time, Ephesus was one of the world's most important cities, and it was home to a goddess cult and the Temple of Artemis. Its magic fascinated other nations, and its merchants were the world's wealthiest, their god the god of materialism.

If Mary lived in Ephesus she was aware of the many pilgrims who journeyed from afar to visit the Temple of Artemis and enjoy other pagan treasures. The city was a modern-day version of Hollywood, host to pleasure hunters, flute players, dancers, and glamorous women. They wore ceremonial garments and dressed like mythical creatures that were part beast and part human.

The mission of early Christianity had been to replace such dangerous paganism with the Gospels of Jesus. Ephesus was treacherous territory and whether or not Mary spent time in that city, she was probably aware of its evils. Most likely her mission was to pray and encourage the disciples, and perhaps they brought back accounts of their travels as she awaited them in Jerusalem.

We are not certain how long the Blessed Mother lived. Some say she died 13 years after Jesus (meaning she was about 61), while others believe she lived into her seventies. Nor do we know what she looked like. Her appearance is sheer guesswork. If an early writer named Epiphanus was correct, she had brown eyes and dark eyebrows. Her face was rather oval, and she probably lived in a small hillside house, eating fruit, fish, and bread. She was of medium height, her complexion the color of wheat, her clothing linen or wool (depending on the season), feet bare or in wood sandals, a veil over her head if she went into the streets, and also wearing a robe or gown.

Some of that concurs with the earliest Christian art,

including Byzantine-like paintings of the Madonna that are claimed to have come from the hand of Luke the Apostle. Legend has it that Luke once painted her image on the top of a wood table and also carved small statues of her.

Since Mary was part of their prayer group, it is likely she continued to pray with the disciples long after the Pentecost. In addition to John and Luke, she must have known John's brother James. We recall that James was with John and their father Zebedee mending nets on a boat when Jesus called to them (see *Matthew* 4:21).

From then on, James was one of the "sons of thunder," a close disciple of Our Savior and as such he witnessed some of Christ's greatest moments, including the Transfiguration (*Matthew* 17:3), the healing of Jairus's daughter (*Mark* 5:23 and *Luke* 8:50), and the agony at Gethsemane.

James was no minor saint and after Jesus died it is believed this apostle traveled as far as Spain and Portugal. On the way it is said he stopped to see the Virgin and implore her prayers. According to legend Mary prayed with James just as she had prayed with him and the other disciples in the Upper Room (*Acts* 1:14) and it's said that Jesus appeared to His mother and promised help for the apostle, explaining that He would transport her to Spain in order to encourage him.

The apostle was having a hard time. Spain was a semi-barbaric territory, inhabited by strange bands of men who were very hostile to outsiders. And it was a bastion of paganism. The passage between the Pillars of Hercules (now called Gibraltar) led to what poets called an impassable sea of darkness. For ancients it had been considered the edge of the world.

One evening, after a particularly difficult and probably dangerous day of evangelizing, James was praying and resting with his own disciples along the Ebro River when he was jarred by a flash of light and the sounds of a heavenly choir. Angels! They were chanting, *"Ave Maria, gratia plena."* James fell to his knees, ravished by the sight of the Virgin Mary descending from the sky seated on a pillar or throne of light, surrounded by angels kneeling on clouds just as Jesus was transported by clouds (see *Acts* 1:9).

Mary then spoke:

"James, servant of the Most High, blessed be thou by God, and may He fill thee with His divine grace. My son James, the Most High and Mighty God of Heaven has chosen this place that you may consecrate and dedicate here a church and house of prayer where, under the invocation of my name, He wishes to be adored and served, and all the faithful who seek my intercession will receive the graces they ask if they have true faith and devotion, and in the Name of my Son I promise them great favors and blessings, for this will be my chapel and my house, my own inheritance and possession, and in testimony of my promise, this pillar will remain here, and on it my own image, which, in this place where you will build my church, will last and endure with the holy faith. Note well this pillar on which I am seated, which my Son and your Master sent down to me from on high by the heads of angels and around which you shall set up the altar of my chapel. On this spot the Most High will work miracles through my intercession for those who implore my protection in their need. And this pillar will remain in this place until the end of the world."

We see that Jesus was at the center of this apparition, as He is always at the center of an authentic apparition. He had empowered Mary through the Holy Spirit. He was behind the miracle. We're not sure if it was an apparition of the Virgin or a case of bilocation. If Mary was still alive, it was bilocation; if she had passed on, it was an apparition. When we go so far back in time, we can't be sure of dates. It's claimed that Mary gave James a small column of jasper upon which was a small but beautiful statue of herself carved in wood and holding the Child Jesus. Others say the statue came later. The Virgin requested that a shrine or church be built on the site, and James constructed a tiny one just 16 feet long and eight feet wide.

It was small, but it was of overwhelming significance. For it was the beginning of Mary's mission to replace pagan temples with Christian ones. One day a huge domed basilica would stand there—the precise size of the Temple of Artemis in Ephesus.

But this temple was dedicated not to a pagan mother-goddess but to the humble Mother of the One True God.

According to the earliest accounts, James gave thanks for the grace and at the end of that apparition watched as the Virgin, accompanied by angels, vanished with them into the clouds. Before leaving she had prophesied that James would return to Jerusalem and die the holy death of a martyr, and indeed this came to be during a persecution of early Christians under King Herod Agrippa I. During James' trial his prosecutor was so impressed by the apostle's steadfast faith that he himself converted. As James was led to execution with the former prosecutor, James embraced his accuser, forgave him, and said "Peace be with you." They were then beheaded together! This took place in Jerusalem but legend says his body was eventually returned to Spain and buried at the famous site of Compostela, which along with Saragossa was to become one of Christianity's greatest shrines.

Many churches have been built at the site of Mary's apparition, withstanding wars and desecrations. Never has paganism polluted it. Never has war destroyed it. Today the huge basilica dominates Saragossa's aging skyline, marking the birthplace of the Spanish Church. From here Christianity would blossom with a fervor known only in a few other nations. To visit this church is to feel Mary's grace—the grace allotted her by Christ—and to encounter an edifice of monumental beauty. There are frescoes by the likes of Goya, and tall, majestic towers. The statue of Mary with Jesus is carved in the Gothic style and stands on the sacred column of jasper, from which issues the odor of sanctity. Our Lady is carved out of dark resinous wood and is usually decorated in a heavy and splendiferous cloth.

A great peace comes upon those who recite the Rosary near this statue, and there are also miracles. The greatest may have occurred in 1640. It involved a young man from Arragon named Michael Juan Pellicer Blasco, whose right leg had been crushed by a wagon and had to be amputated just below the knee. Blasco had a great devotion to Our Lady of the Pillar, and after his operation would often visit the Saragossa basilica, anointing his stump with oil from one of the lamps that burned before the Blessed Virgin. While he still suffered from the accident, Blasco gave thanks to Mary for saving his life and was often seen in front of the church begging for money.

On March 29, 1640, Blasco had an amazing dream. In it he found himself roaming the interior of the basilica and anointing his stump with the oil. At about eleven that night his mother entered his room and noticed two feet at the end of his bed, instead of the usual one. At first she thought it must be someone else using the bed, perhaps one of the soldiers quartered in town. But no. It was her son. It was Michael. She ran to get her husband, and they awoke Michael—whose amputated leg somehow had been regenerated!

We would dismiss such a seemingly implausible account but for the credible witnesses. Many told authorities that they had seen the one-legged beggar, and there were records of the amputation at Grace Hospital in Saragossa by two surgeons named D. Millaruelo and J. Estanga. The leg was buried by an assistant whose name was also in the records. At a hearing initiated by the city government, a couple dozen people offered formal testimony and on April 27, 1641, Archbishop P. Apolaza formally declared it a miracle. Pope Urban VIII was notified.

Thus we see that the most astounding physiological effects—even regeneration of a limb!—can be accomplished through the intercession of Mary. She had come to Spain to replace paganism, and so we, in our lives, should look to cleanse hidden areas of darkness. We should seek to purify our society. As we pray, we should ask the Holy Spirit to let us realize our evil and purge it. We should seek God's help in purifying ourselves of past sins, of lust, of deception, of anger. We should ask the Lord to cleanse us of any occultism just as Mary cleansed Saragossa—and soon the rest of Europe—of paganism. Her feast day is October 12.

Meditation

Lord Jesus, You are the Holy One, You are the Most High, You are our Creator. We beg of Thee, O Lord, to come into the very foundation of our beings and give us insight on how to live our lives. Grant us such affection of the heart that we see all things through the eyes of love and never grow angry. O Lord, let us shed all bad habits. Let us never sin again. Let us form ourselves in perfect union with You, living for You and You alone. Let us operate every waking moment with charity.

Cleanse us of all impurity, O Lord. Form our very beings according to Thy Will. Be our only foundation. Please, O Lord; please, Holy Spirit; please, Lord Christ: come into and around our lives. Guide our every thought and action. Let it be a sure way to Heaven. Let it be a new beginning. Let this be a new awakening for us.

Come, Holy Spirit. Come, Lord Christ. Come as You came to Saragossa, as You showed James Your splendor, as You gave him Your mother, and grant to us her signal graces as well as the light of truth which comes from Thee.

Grant us truth, O Lord. Let us evaluate our lives in Your Light. Let us see all our faults and through Your grace correct them. O Jesus, O Lord: come to us as You sent Your mother to James and help us in our daily struggles. O dear Lord, teach us how to view ourselves. Teach us how to view one another.

Teach us how to view life. Teach us, dear Lord, how to approach every minute so that one day, in our last minute, we may sing with the angels.

O Holy Spirit, come into the fibers of our being. Erase all evil. Teach us how to pray. Be with us every minute and every second of the rest of our lives, and let us move forward as James did and bring Your Word to heathen territories.

O Jesus, O Holy Spirit, O Mighty God, pervade our beings so that we may be exactly the person You wanted each of us to be. Grant us grace as if we too had been present at the Transfiguration and with You at Gethsemane and witnesses of Your Resurrection. Grant us the sweet feeling James had upon seeing the image of Mary on the cloud with her angels.

Pray for us, sweet Virgin, as you prayed with the apostles in the Upper Room. Enter our lives as you entered James' life. Let us live our lives simply. Let us be content with the basics. Let us never be persuaded by the glamour of this passing world. Form our very beings, form our way of worship, form our society as you formed the early Church.

Dear Lord, let us take into this first day the pleasant blessing of Saragossa. Let us feel as if we are praying there at the great basilica. Let us feel as if we are there in front of the miraculous statue. Grant us peace, O Holy Spirit. Lift up our spirits. Wash away anxiety and discouragement as You washed it away from James.

And like James let us go forth without fear knowing that this life is a life to be lived for You, Lord Jesus, for You, Holy Spirit, for You, Lord God, and You alone.

Let us pray (response: pray for us)

O Virgin, who intervened at the very beginning of the
   Christian age,
O Virgin, who comes when we call,
O Virgin of purity,

O Virgin of prayer,
O Virgin, who gave James strength,
O Virgin, who will also grant us strength,
O Virgin, through whom Christ performs many
    healings,
O Virgin, spouse of the Holy Spirit,
O Virgin, who shows us her Son,
    Pray for us!

As the angels prayed at Saragossa so too do we pray

Ave Maria, gratia plena,
Dominus tecum. Benedicta tu in mulieribus,
et benedictus fructus ventris tui, Jesus.
Sancta Maria, Mater Dei,
ora pro nobis peccatoribus,
nunc, et in hora mortis nostra.
Amen.

And as Pope John Paul II has prayed

O Mary,
Bright dawn of the new world,
Mother of the living,
to you do we entrust the cause of life:
Look down, O Mother,
upon the vast numbers
of babies to be born,
of the poor whose lives are made difficult,
of men and women
who are victims of brutal violence,
of the elderly and the sick killed
by indifference or out of misguided mercy.
Grant that all who believe in your Son
may proclaim the Gospel of life

with honesty and love
to the people in our time.
Obtain for them the grace
to accept that Gospel
as a gift ever new,
the joy of celebrating it with gratitude
throughout our lives
and the courage to bear witness to it
resolutely, in order to build,
together with all people of good will,
the civilization of truth and love,
to the praise and glory of God,
the Creator and Lover of life. Amen.

Ejaculation

O Lord, Who deigned to cause a miracle at
Saragossa, Who purged Spain of paganism, purge our
society too of occultism and evil.
Pray with us Blessed Mother as you prayed with James.
Heal us as you healed the beggar named Blasco.
Be with us, sweet Virgin, Our Lady of Saragossa, at
every crossroad in our lives.

Spanish prayer from Saragossa

Glorious Virgin of the Pillar, your compassion for the
Hispanic people encouraged the Apostle James and encourages
us in all adversities and dangers that surround us. Pour upon us
the abundance of your mercy and give us the spiritual and
temporal graces that we need to serve God and you in this life
and the life to come. Amen. (*Followed by a Hail Mary in
memory of Mary's coming to Saragossa; a Hail Mary in
thanksgiving for all her blessings; and a Hail Mary for her
protection.*)

Another prayer from Saragossa

Glorious Virgin of the Pillar, you visited our patron James, and you assured him that the Catholic Faith will never leave this sacred place. Give us, we humbly pray, the same assurance against the indifference and impiety and protestation, and under your guidance lead us to recover the Catholic unity that in the past was the crown of Spain. Amen

A generational prayer

Mary, God chose you as the mother of His Son and called all nations and generations to bless the gift of grace He gave you. In the company of those who have gone before us, with people of all races and languages, we call upon you in prayer.

Litany (response : pray for us)

Holy Mary,
Mother of God,
Mother of our redemption,
Mother of the lost Child,
Mother of comfort and understanding,
Mother who shares our joys,
Mother who endures our sorrows,
Mother whose heart was pierced by a sword,
Mother most mercilful,

Mary, you are mother and virgin, wife and widow, peasant and queen, blessed for all time. We need the comfort of your prayers. Remember us always to our Father through your Son, Jesus Christ, Who is our Lord forever and ever. Amen.

The Salve Regina

Hail, holy Queen, Mother of Mercy, our life, our sweetness, and our hope! To you we cry, poor banished children of Eve; to you we send up our sighs, mourning and weeping in this valley of tears. Turn then, most gracious advocate, your eyes of mercy toward us; and after this our exile, show to us the blessed fruit of your womb, Jesus. O clement, O loving, O sweet Virgin Mary:
    Pray for us, O holy Mother of God.
    That we may be made worthy of the promises of Christ.

Angelus

V: The angel spoke God's message to Mary
R: And she conceived of the Holy Spirit.
    (*Hail Mary, full of grace...*)
V: "I am the lowly servant of the Lord:
R: Let it be done to me according to your word."
    (*Hail Mary...*)
V: And the Word became flesh
R: and dwelt amongst us.
    (*Hail Mary...*)
V: Pray for us, holy Mother of God,
R: That we may become worthy of the promises of Christ.

Let us pray: Lord, fill our hearts with Your grace: once, through the message of an angel, You revealed to us the incarnation of Your Son; now, through His suffering and death, lead us to the glory of His Resurrection. We ask this through Christ our Lord. Amen.

Prayer of St. Alphonsus

Behold, O Mother of God, at thy feet a miserable sinner, a slave of Hell, who has recourse to thee and trusts in thee. I do not deserve that thou shouldst even look at me; but I know that thou, having seen thy Son die for the salvation of sinners, hast the greatest desire to help them. I hear all call thee the refuge of sinners, the hope of those who are in despair, and the help of the abandoned. Thou art, then, my refuge, my hope, and my help. Thou hast to save me by thy intercession. Help me, for the love of Jesus Christ; extend thy hand to a miserable creature who has fallen and recommends himself to thee.

Contemplation

All of life is a preparation for the afterlife, sweet Virgin. We here beg that you help us keep our eyes on Heaven, that you guide our every act and thought and deed, that you orient and prepare us so that immediately upon death we may find the glory of the radiant clouds and angels as seen at Saragossa; the glory of Heaven.

(Ending with recitation of the daily Rosary)

Second Day

Our Lady of Montserrat

The surprisingly early history of Mary was also demonstrated in places like France, where the Virgin appeared to an infirm woman at a place called Le Puy, and her intercession was seen at numerous sites in Italy, where she continued to quash and replace pagan idols. Christian churches were erected where once demons had been worshipped and Christ continued to employ His mother as a vessel for His wonders, His deliverance.

There were few messages in these early days. When Mary spoke, it was just a few terse sentences. She was quiet. She was sublime. When she spoke it was with very few words, and usually those words were a request to build a church. Truly she was the Mother of the Church in both a spiritual and actual fashion. Hundreds of shrines, churches, and basilicas were built at her behest as she worked to bring Europe out of the horrible grip of idolatry. She was the woman in *Genesis* who crushes the head of the serpent.

This might come as a shock to those who believe that devotion to Mary is a recent fad. It assuredly is not. It is at the foundation of traditional Christianity. For twenty centuries she has healed. She has helped the impoverished.

And she has worked to save souls. That has always been her main mission. It is not philosophy. It is not politics. The Virgin knows that our earthly life is a fleeting one, and as a good mother, as the kindest mother, as the dearest of all mothers, she comes gently but with force to guide us onto a path that brings us closer to eternal happiness.

In the early days she often did this through miraculous images, including the ones claimed to have been carved or painted by Luke. According to legend, Luke painted Mary while she was staying in the home of John, using the top of a table that had been built by Jesus in His father's workshop. As he painted, according to this account, Mary related details of the life of Jesus, details that were later recorded in Luke's Gospel. The painting was supposedly discovered by St. Helena (mother of Constantine the Great) in the fourth century, and eventually found its way through Ukraine to Poland, where it was damaged through the ages and eventually repainted on new canvas but backed with the original wooden boards. Historians have never been able to verify such ancient facts, but there are those who believe the portrait is behind the famous image of Czestochowa.

There were many such images, and they were an important way for Heaven to communicate with humans. Just as we photograph loved ones, so did Heaven want us to have remembrances of Jesus and His mother. There have always been special graces with such images because they invoke a heavenly blessing. Those who confuse such images with idolatry do so because they confuse heavenly images with those of demonic creatures. That's a shame, because holy images have been an important vehicle of Christian evangelization for two millennia. At the end of the sixth century Pope Gregory the Great used one such image to ward off a plague!

There is intercession with Mary's images and one of the

most vivid examples is the one we focus upon today. It is known as Montserrat. It too is an ancient image—the original may likewise have dated to the earliest centuries—and it is called Montserrat after a towering mountain by that name. Far up the incredible highland, which looks like massive sawed-off stone, is a monastery and church containing a slender statue of Mary in a sitting position, darkened by the smoke of candles and holding the globe in one hand as Jesus sits on her lap.

It is a most mysterious image, the Virgin's face elongated, her head crowned with a diadem and wearing a tunic and golden mantle. It's located in an alcove high above the church behind the main altar, accessible to the pilgrim by a narrow stairway that takes one onto a step allowing the actual touching of the relic.

The image is known as the "Little Dark Lady of Montserrat" and also *La Jerosolimitana,* or "Native of Jerusalem," for peasants in the region repeat the legend that this statue represents one of those carved by Luke and brought to Spain in the first century.

Once more there's no way of knowing the exact origin but what we know is that Montserrat is one of the world's holiest and most august sanctuaries. As long ago as April 22, 718, there was word of a statue in the area of Barcelona that like so many others had to be hidden from Arab invaders. The hiding place had been a cave where the image remained hidden for two centuries. There were already holy men high up the mountain, hermitages that in the words of one writer were "built on impossible ledges and on incredibly high places, situated like eagles' eyries," transforming the peaks—the enormous blocks and crags—into altars of perpetual adoration. There was no holier place outside of Jerusalem and by 888 a hermitage called "Santa Maria" was in existence, overlooking the vast expanses of emerging Europe below.

The image of Our Blessed Mother remained hidden until 890, when some local boys spotted a strange light coming from the eastern part of the mountain. It was near the cave. They described the light as like that of many candles, descending from Heaven, and as they approached, these boys, like James before them, heard the sound of music and canticles. It was a Saturday, and the boys quickly informed the local priest in the village of Monistrol. The priest didn't believe them at first and wanted to see for himself. When he ventured up Montserrat he was stunned to see the lights and hear the inexplicable music. The boys were right! There was a miracle on that mountain! The priest informed the Bishop of Manresa, who also headed for the site, followed by a procession of villagers.

"The canticles, the lights, and the fragrant aroma that rose from this mysterious place affected the people so much that the bishop, filled with the deepest devotion, ordered that the cave be entered, and there they found the image which had been a fount of miracles and an object of universal veneration," wrote Jose Maria de Sagarra in a book about Montserrat. "The bishop wanted to take such a wonderful treasure to his cathedral at Manresa, but when those who were carrying the Virgin reached this place where today the monastery rises, they found that they could not move a single step backwards or forwards, and this new miracle was interpreted as a sign that the Virgin desired her sanctuary to be erected on that very spot, as was done."

I was shocked upon visiting Montserrat not only at its awesome, majestic height (4,055 feet), not only at the beauty of the monastery's incredible gold-gilded basilica, not only at the fantasy setting, but also at the tangible graces that exude from the wood statue, which is about three feet tall.

This miraculous image, believed to be a replacement of the original, is Romanesque in style and is said to date to the 12th century. It has that dark Byzantine look to the face and the aura surrounding it leaves the pilgrims in reverential awe.

The Virgin, at the heights of a mountain; the Virgin in a high place just as Christ went to Mount Tabor—a high place—

17

to communicate with Heaven.

The Virgin, holding the world.

It's not clear why mountains have spiritual significance, but since Moses this has proven to be the case and there is no better example of a holy mountain outside of Israel than Montserrat. A drive to the monastery is several harrowing and spectacular miles around the mountain and is located more than midway up at 2,846 feet.

Some say it is among the best candidates for former sanctuaries of the Holy Grail.

Among visitors through the ages have been Jaime I, known as *El Conquistador*; Fernando I; St. Vincent Ferrer; and St. Ignatius Loyola, who divested his clothes and gave them to a poor man after a pilgrimage to Montserrat, writing his famous spiritual exercises in a cave in nearby Manresa.

Few doubt the influence the Black Virgin had on Ignatius, who embarked on his new mission to found an order, the Jesuits, after spending a night in prayer before the image.

King Louis IV prayed here, and one of Montserrat's hermits accompanied Christopher Columbus, who dedicated one of the first churches in the New World to the Virgin of Montserrat, where an island today bears the name.

So too did Montserrat produce an abbot named Giuliano ella Rovere, who became the pope who hired Michelangelo.

As an emperor named Carlos V said, "a certain divinity which I cannot explain" flows from the sanctuary of Montserrat all over the mountain.

Prominent in the history is the account of a hermit who fell into temptation, murdered the daughter of a famous count, and as a result was transformed by God into the shaggy body of a beast until he was forgiven.

Whatever the merits of such legends, they point up the mercy and forgiveness of God. They point out His heights. They point out His mystery. I cannot more highly recommend a sanctuary than Montserrat. I was truly surprised by the strength of its effect. I was impressed by the atmosphere of holiness way up that unique mountain and what it teaches us about praying in solitude.

And so we meditate

O Virgin Mary, you who have sent us your images so that we can feel the atmosphere of Heaven, so that we can taste a bit of paradise, so that we can better pray in church, please also send forth this atmosphere in our homes and lives. Let us have in our daily living the kind of grace that emanates from Montserrat, that we may always see with spiritual eyes and always keep our eyes high above the clouds.

Yes, O sweet Virgin of Montserrat, grant by the power of your Son that we may have the same expansive view, the spiritual sight, afforded at the heights of Montserrat, and that we may feel the power and expediency and consolation that is felt by those who touch your image in the basilica.

Let us feel that now. Let us touch the image. Let us transcend all storms of life as you transcend at Montserrat. Guide us on the mission assigned to us by Jesus and be with us on our journeys as you guided pilgrims of the past, as you guided St. Ignatius, as you guided kings and popes and bishops. Come O holy Virgin in a new and special way and guard us against the temptations of this world, the lust that always threatens to overtake us, the materialism that runs rampant around us.

Guard us, holy Virgin, against the deceits of this world.

And when we do sin, let us find the mercy of God and our way back to full grace, as did that legendary hermit.

Let us always find our way back to faith.

Let us always have you as a special and ancient friend.

O Holy Spirit, shed Your Light that we may see our hidden sins and faults and may ever appreciate Your intercession. Let us forsake all wrongful passion and lust and greed and anger and negativity, let us know when we are in error, let us never believe we are beyond temptation but rather be prepared for all the lures of this ensnaring and illusory world.

Sweet Mary, teach us to make good and regular confession that we may one day come before your Son as pure. While on earth, surround us with your angels and let our souls flow pure and aloft.

Let us pray (response: pray for us)

O Virgin of the heights in this world,
O Virgin of ancient miracles,
O Virgin, who gives us insight,
O Virgin, who lifts the spiritual blinders,
O Virgin, who ministers with music,
O Virgin, who always comes with light,
O Virgin, who has formed so many holy men and women,
O Virgin, who oversaw the development of Europe,
O Virgin, who also oversaw the New World,
O Virgin, who withstood all the assaults of the early
    centuries,
O Virgin, who inspires popes,
    Pray for us.

Ancient prayer to the Virgin Mary

We turn to you for protection,
holy Mother of God.
Listen to our prayers
and help us in our needs.
Save us from every danger,
glorious and blessed Virgin.

Litany of Mary of Nazareth

Glory to You, God our Creator
Breathe into us new life, new meaning.
Glory to You, God our Savior.
Lead us in the way of peace and justice.
Glory to You, healing Spirit.
Transform us to empower others.
Mary, wellspring of peace,
Be our guide
Model of strength
Model of gentleness
Model of trust
Model of courage
Model of patience
Model of risk
Model of openness
Model of perseverance
Mother of the Liberator
   Pray for us.

Consecration through Mary

O Immaculate Mary, O Virgin of Montserrat, I, a faithless sinner, renew and ratify today in thy hands the vows of my Baptism; I renounce forever Satan, his pomp and works; and I give myself entirely to Jesus Christ, the Incarnate Wisdom, to carry my cross after Him all the days of my life, and to be more faithful to Him than I have ever been before. In the presence of all the heavenly court I choose this day my Mother and Mistress. I deliver and consecrate to thee, as they slave, my body and soul, my goods, both interior and exterior, and even the value of all my actions, past, present, and future; leaving to thee the entire and full right of disposing of me, and all that belongs to me, without exception, according to thy good

21

pleasure, for the greater glory of God, in time and in eternity.

Consecration to Jesus the Incarnate Wisdom through the Blessed Virgin Mary

O Eternal and Incarnate Wisdom. O sweetest and most adorable Jesus. True God and true man, only Son of the Eternal Father, and of Mary, always Virgin. I adore Thee profoundly in the bosom and splendors of Thy Father during eternity; and I adore Thee also in the virginal bosom of Mary, Thy most worthy Mother, in the time of Thine Incarnation. I give Thee thanks for that Thou hast annihilated Thyself, taking the form of a slave in order to rescue me from the cruel slavery of the devil. I dare not come by myself before Thy most holy and august majesty. It is on this account that I have recourse to the intercession of Thy most holy Mother, whom Thou hast given me for a mediatrix with Thee. It is through her that I hope to obtain of Thee contrition, the pardon of my sins, and the acquisition and preservation of wisdom. Hail then, O Immaculate Mary, living tabernacle of the Divinity, where the Eternal Wisdom willed to be hidden and to be adored by angels and men. Receive, O benignant Virgin, this little offering of my slavery, in honor of, and in union with, that subjection which the Eternal Wisdom deigned to have to thy maternity, in homage to the power which both of you have over this poor sinner, and in thanksgiving for the privileges with which the Holy Trinity has favored thee, I declare that I wish henceforth, as they true slave, to seek thy honor and to obey thee in all things.

Angelus

V: The angel spoke God's message to Mary
R: And she conceived of the Holy Spirit.
   (*Hail Mary, full of grace. . .*)

V: "I am the lowly servant of the Lord:
R: Let it be done to me according to your word."
   (*Hail Mary. . .*)
V: And the Word became flesh
R: and dwelt amongst us.
   (*Hail Mary. . .*)
V: Pray for us, holy Mother of God,
R: That we may become worthy of the promises of
   Christ.

Let us pray: Lord, fill our hearts with Your grace: once, through the message of an angel, You revealed to us the incarnation of Your Son; now, through His suffering and death, lead us to the glory of His resurrection. We ask this through Christ our Lord. Amen.

Contemplation

However much the world tempts us, we know that it is a passing place and that if we do good, if we help others—most of all, if we are reverential, if we love and serve Christ, and if we are humble, hidden as the Virgin's statue was hidden—we will resurface, as at Montserrat, in glory.

Prayer of St. Alphonsus

O Queen of Heaven, I, who was once a miserable slave of Lucifer, now dedicate myself to thee, to be thy servant forever; I offer myself to honor thee and serve thee during my whole life; do thou accept me, and refuse me not, as I should deserve. O my Mother, in thee have I placed all my hopes, from thee do I expect every grace.

(*Ending with recitation of the Rosary*)

Third Day

Our Lady of Good Counsel

If Spain was a hotspot for Mary's wonders, it was no more so than Italy, where shrines dedicated to the Virgin Mary had a deep and rich past. To try and catalogue all the miraculous sites in Italy would be an impossible task. On mountain after mountain, in shrine after shrine, with peasant after peasant, the Virgin showed herself to help construction of yet more churches and to save mankind from chastisements like the plague.

One could spend years visiting all of Mary's Italian sites, and Our Lady of Good Counsel ranks with the best of them. The power here, the grace with this particular image—the wonder of the incredible miracle—knows no bounds.

Located about 30 miles southeast of Rome in a town called Genazzano, Good Counsel can trace its history to the fifth century. It was then, during the reign of Sixtus III, that a church was built and named *Madre nostra del Buon Consiglio*. The name derived from the writings of St. Augustine, and the placement of Good Counsel was of great significance, for it was at a location that during earlier times had been the scene of orgies and ceremonies dedicated to Venus (the "love goddess").

Now Mary—the pure Virgin, so opposite a goddess—was moving in to take the territory back for Jesus. We saw how this happened at Saragossa, and now it happened again, the Mother of God pushing aside the mother-goddess of sin and lust. In the words of one historian, it was Providence which had arranged "that the mother and synonym of vice which, with other dark and sorrowful characters, has folly emphatically stamped upon it, should be succeeded, when faith shed its light upon Latium, by the Mother and synonym of purity and supernal wisdom, the Mother of 'fair love' and of 'holy hope,' of consolation and of counsel."

This church that had defeated paganism at Genazzano served Christianity for 1,000 years but eventually fell into ruins. It was a little church and was overshadowed by more splendid edifices dedicated to St. John and St. Nicholas. In time there was just about nothing left of the ancient sanctuary, which greatly upset a pious woman named Petruccia de Geneo, whose husband had been caretaker of the Augustinians in town. He had died in 1436, and with what money he left, Petruccia set about providing certain basic necessities for the church and vowed to rebuild the entire dilapidated edifice.

Many were amused at Petruccia's ambitious designs and indeed she wasn't able to get much further than rough and unfinished walls for the church's chapel. Her money had quickly run out, and few were those to support her efforts. Yet Petruccia insisted she had been assured by the Virgin Mother that against all logic the church would be rebuilt.

When townsfolk mocked Petruccia to scorn, pointing out that the restoration was woefully incomplete, Petruccia responded patiently. "My children, don't take such notice of this apparent misfortune, for I assure you that before I die the Most Blessed Virgin and the holy father St. Augustine will complete the church."

These were words of faith *and the prophecy was true.*

Petruccia's faith was about to be rewarded in a way that no one, in wildest imaginings, could have foretold.

The date was the feast day, April 25, 1467. Though the church remained in a state of disintegration, many went to celebrate the day of Good Counsel—as they always had—in the nearby plaza or "*piazza*" of Santa Maria, having clean fun where once there had been the baths and decadence of pagan idols.

"During the festival, the piazza of Santa Maria, adjoining the church, was always the most frequented," wrote a later historian, Monsignor George F. Dillon. "Some attended its stalls and booths, and others its amusements, while all were at the same time within easy reach of the temple and its ministers."

This year the crowd was especially dense, owing to the fact that April 25 fell on a Saturday. At about 4 p.m. the crowd in the Plaza of Saint Mary was astonished to hear what sounded like a celestial harmony, which reminds us of the heavenly choirs reported at both Montserrat and Saragossa. It was high in the clouds, the music of angels, as if a portal or opening to paradise had been flung open. Such descriptions come from Church historians like Monsignor Dillon, who explains that soon those in the throngs spotted an unusual and beautiful cloud above the church's lofty turrets.

It makes us think back to the strange wispy cloud that Elijah's servant witnessed (*1 Kings* 18:44) and also the cloud that took Jesus to Heaven (*Acts* 1:9). It is said that the cloud was a beautiful white and sent forth vivid rays of light. It lowered and to the amazement of the assembled people rested upon the unfinished wall of the church's chapel, which was dedicated to Saint Biagio.

"Suddenly the bells of the high campanile, which stood before their eyes, began to peal, though they saw and knew that no human hand touched them," wrote Monsignor Dillon. "And then, in unison, every church bell in the town began to answer in peals as festive. The crowd was spellbound, ravished, and yet full of holy feeling. With eager haste they filled the enclosure; they pressed around the spot where the cloud remained. Gradually the rays of light ceased to dart, the cloud began to clear gently away, and then, to their astonishment, there remained disclosed *a most beautiful object.*"

There was a physical object in the midst of the cloud.

It was an image of the Blessed Virgin holding Jesus in her arms.

Another miraculous image.

As if to materialize from nowhere.

Mary was not portrayed as a beauty queen, not like a high-fashion model, but instead exuded a *spiritual* beauty. She showed a concern and tenderness as she held the Infant. It was as if she was looking into the future and knew the tests of mankind and the fate of her beloved Son.

In a word, there was tremendous *caring*. Mary emphasized her role as a warm but serious mother. If at Saragossa she was the consolation of evangelists, and if at Montserrat she emphasized her influence on Church leaders like Ignatius, at Genazzano she showed herself as mother to every single person and she did so on a level that was tremendously individual.

The image of Good Counsel as well as subsequent reproductions demonstrate a warmth that touches the most profound depths of our spirits. They indicate that in our greatest difficulties we can flee with great confidence into the warmth of Mary. She is the Mother of God but also Mother of us all. Imbued by the Holy Spirit, the Virgin knows each of the six billion people on earth and knows each one better than anyone knows himself! The tenderness she has is because her perspective is different from ours. She knows our innermost trials. She knows what we were born with. She knows what we have overcome and what we still need to overcome. She can gauge the challenges we have faced in a way we simply cannot do with human consciousness.

Mary's eyes are Heaven's eyes. They are *maternal* eyes. And her beauty is her warmth. As she looks down toward the Infant she holds, so too does she look down to all the people on earth, caring for them, concerned for them, knowing the many struggles.

The sensitivity and yet the strength in the Genazzano image mesmerized all who set eyes upon it. Jesus has his right arm around his mother's neck and the left hand on her neckline hem. He is clinging to her in the most touching way, and while the Madonna appeared sad from some angles, from other perspectives she appeared to smile. Her features, especially her arched brows, her eyes, and the contour of her long slender nose, remind us a bit of Byzantine madonnas such as Czestochowa or Our Lady of Kazan. When later it was measured, the picture of Good Counsel was about 16 by 18 inches.

Most miraculously, the painting did not seem to have any normal means of support. It was a fresco done on a thin layer of plaster or porcelain, rather much like an eggshell. There is no way such an image could be transported any distance without ruin, and no way it could stand on its own, but that is precisely what had happened: the image was resting only on its base, supported by nothing in the front, at its back, or on top. It just *balanced* there—and does so to this day.

"*Evviva Maria! Evviva Maria!*" some shouted, while other yelled. "Miracle! A miracle!"

A great miracle, a great sign, indeed, and one that is with us through the centuries, for even while the wheels of wagons and now modern-day vehicles may cause vibrations in the church, causing silver lamps to budge, it is said the delicate image never trembles.

We can imagine how swiftly word spread that a wonder had occurred in the church that poor Petruccia—never losing faith—had tried to resurrect. And soon the church was springing back to life in a way that would place it above all but a few holy places, with graces comparable to anywhere in Italy or for that matter the world. The sick and depressed and distressed hurried to the run-down chapel, first from neighboring towns, then from communities far away. Entire villages emptied of their inhabitants as word of the great sign from Heaven was disseminated.

It was one of many intercessions by Mary in the Middle Ages. Time and again she had been invoked to ward off plague and often a miracle was attached to a painting, fresco, or statue. Heaven had anointed such images, which were representations of the new covenant of Jesus, Who Himself had given mankind a visual representation of God. Where before mankind had committed the sin of worshipping *idolatrous* images (of snakes and other vile things), these holy images, these images of holy figures, were Heaven's way of sweeping away the lingering and always resurfacing paganism.

At Genazzano hundreds of people remained prostrate before the image through the night and there were many solemn processions in the days and nights after the miracle. It was comparable to the great sign that later happened at Fatima. Hundreds and then thousands witnessing a supernatural occurrence! And it was no idle wonder. It was not a standard miracle. It was a sign that the humble and immaculate Virgin had overcome the spirit of pride, debauchery, and lust just as she comes to us in our everyday lives and sweeps away similar filth.

Needless to say that after the miracle the church was promptly rebuilt as Petruccia had prophesied. No one could deny the wonder. In the four months after arrival of the unfathomable object, 171 miraculous healings were recorded and this led to official Church recognition of Good Counsel. To this day the colors and details on the painting remain inexplicably fresh. In the picture Jesus has a look that tugs at our hearts, a look that has been described by writers like Dillon as anxious fondness. He holds onto His mother in a way that indicates He too knows what He must endure, and while showing no fear, He has natural seriousness about His incredible mission.

"Nowhere else, not even in the Eternal City, the metropolis of art, is the Adorable Infant so powerfully and, apparently, so perfectly portrayed, so as to appear not only willing but anxious to relieve the sorrow which His mother endured for His sake, by granting every prayer she may offer," wrote Monsignor Dillon.

The picture exudes modesty and dignity. And while there is anxious concern, there is also phenomenal strength. The Infant appears to be girding His mother, giving her strength and courage. Her eyebrows are arching. Her oval face is tilted. Those who view this picture that seems to defy gravity claim it changes colors depending on the season of the year, and it was discovered that an identical image disappeared right around the time of the miracle from a church in Scutari, Albania, that was under assault by Turks. In other words, it appeared to have been miraculously transported from one nation to another, just as the house at Loreto was transported.

Those who seek favor from Mary say the image seems to smile when their requests are to be granted. They also say she seems to turn radiant and joyful during Mass, the image assuming new auras of majesty, the cheeks rosier, the eyes not only majestic and full of wisdom but also lighting up, joyful and pleasantly lucid. No one knows exactly when or how the image was originally made. One well-known Italian painter commented in 1747 that "because the features and the delineations, as well of the holy Image of Mary as also of the holy Child, Whom she holds close to her breast and to her face in an attitude graceful and loving, are so fine, delicate, gentle, amiable, and singular, the whole picture seems properly rather an angelic work than a human work."

It is like the colors were celestially impressed, and the

original does not quite fit into the mode of Gothic or Greek nor modern or any famous style. There have been many copies, one of which is on the cover of this book, embellishing the image and beautifying it yet capturing its exquisite humility. The details of its arrival are so seemingly outlandish that had not the image of Good Counsel been so well documented by notaries who were sent to the scene on behalf of the Pope, today we might disregard it as a legend. In the 17th century Pope Urban VIII, who was very strict when it came to accepting miracles, made a famous pilgrimage to Genazzano seeking relief from a pestilence that was devastating Italy. It worked. The plague stopped, just as it had stopped when Gregory the Great paraded an image through Rome. Many blind have received their sight at Genazzano while others have been cured of hearing loss, epileptic affliction, and possession by the devil. The Church has instituted an Office and Mass based upon Good Counsel and several other popes have taken keen interest in this most special place, this place that is so strong against lust, this place where we seek shelter from the foul temptations of this world—this place that teaches us to give up all we have as Petruccia did and move forward in the service of God.

During World War Two a bomb crashed into the basilica and did terrible damage—the altar totally ruined—but a few yards away the delicate image, balancing so inexplicably, was unaffected.

If I may mention my own experience with Our Lady of Good Counsel, it is to say that in the early 1980s, when I was living in the fast-lane of New York City, I was brought back to the faith and converted through a local church on East 90th Street named after Good Counsel.

Later I was to learn that all those years my grandmother had been invoking Our Lady of Good Counsel!

In our confusion, in our debauchery, in our uncleanliness, the Virgin never abandons us but arrives to dispel our darkness.

Surely our society needs the Virgin of Good Counsel at

least as much as they did in Roman times when smoke curled from the hillsides during pagan sacrifices.

And so we meditate

Dear Virgin Mary, who deigned to send a miraculous image to Genazzano, who came in the midst of paganism, who had transformed that place in the earlier centuries from a center of orgies to one of holiness, O please, Blessed Virgin, come with the strength of your purity into our homes and hearts and rid too from our surroundings the poison of this world. O Blessed Virgin, please look into our hearts and once again remove any darkness that lingers, any impurity that remains, any ungodly ambition, and open our eyes to evil in our lives. As you so easily arrived to dispel the darkness of paganism, please do so again in our homes and throughout our pagan society.

As you rebuilt the chapel, please rebuild our Church.

O Blessed Virgin, you in your wisdom know how strong are the temptations of this world. You know, sweet Virgin, how good it can seem to have money, how good it can seem to have prestige, how good it can seem to have pride and worldly honors.

O Blessed Virgin, you know how difficult it can be for us to function in a world that looks upon material possessions as a sign of goodness.

Yet always remind us, Blessed Virgin, that this world is a testing ground and not our real home. Always remind us, O sweet and poor Virgin, that you and Joseph and your Son lived in holy poverty, leaving all in the Hands of the Father, not caring what others thought, not trying to excel in a material way, but rather disdaining the pleasures of this world so that you could attain the heights of the next.

Please, O Virgin, let us work for God as you work for God, and detach us from the vacant glories and honors and fame of the world.

Let all that we do be done for God and God alone.

O Virgin Mary, please counsel us always. Please counsel us as to how to view life and everyday happenings. Please counsel us on how to avoid the pitfalls of money, jealousy, and worldliness. Please counsel us on how to develop great faith as Petruccia had great faith, great trust as Petruccia had great trust, great fervor as those who saw your image had great fervor that incredible day in 1467 when you came to elevate the poorest of churches, the least of churches, as God elevates the least of His children.

O Virgin of Good Counsel, convert those in our families who are caught in the web of this world, in the deceits of drugs or alcohol, in the addiction to television and modern-day orgies. As you came in the very place where there had been pagan baths, come and purify our surroundings, that we may be made worthy of the promises of your Son, Whom you hold so dearly and knowingly at Genazzano.

Let us pray (response: pray for us)

O Mary, who arrives in the hour of poverty,
O Mary, who comes where you are needed most,
O Mary, who responds to our faith,
O Mary, who not only built but also rebuilt the
    Church,
O Mary, who is powerful against the temptations of
    the flesh,
O Mary, who knows that we face our own trials and
    crosses,
O Mary, of Good Counsel, who whispers advice,
    Pray for us.

Angelus

V: The angel spoke God's message to Mary

R: And she conceived of the Holy Spirit.
  (*Hail Mary, full of grace. . .*)
V: "I am the lowly servant of the Lord:
R: Let it be done to me according to your word."
  (*Hail Mary. . .*)
V: And the Word became flesh
R: and dwelt amongst us.
  (*Hail Mary. . .*)
V: Pray for us, holy Mother of God,
R: That we may become worthy of the promises of
  Christ.

Let us pray: Lord, fill our hearts with Your grace: once, through the message of an angel, You revealed to us the incarnation of Your Son; now, through His suffering and death, lead us to the glory of His resurrection. We ask this through Christ our Lord. Amen.

Prayer of Good Counsel

O Mary of Good Counsel, inflame the hearts of all who are devoted to you, so that all of them have shelter in you, O great Mother of God. O most worthy Lady, let everyone choose you as teacher and wise counselor of their souls, since you are, as St. Augustine says, the counsel of the Apostles and counsel of all peoples. Amen.

From the liturgy

—Lord, You know that our thoughts on earth are full of fear and uncertainty; through the intercession of the Blessed Virgin Mary, from whom Your Son took flesh and blood, send us the Spirit of Counsel to teach us how to know Your Will, and to guide us in all we do.

—Grant this through our Lord Jesus Christ, Your Son,

Who lives and reigns with You and the Holy Spirit, one God, forever and ever. Amen.

—Lord, we have shared in Your mysteries on this memorial of Our Lady, Mother of Good Counsel.

—Grant that we may learn what is pleasing to You, and receive salvation from Your Son, Whom You gave to us as our wonderful Counselor through the cooperation of His Blessed Mother. We ask this through Christ our Lord. Amen.

Ejaculation

Mother supreme, who is always there for us, who comes in such miraculous ways, who watches our every plight and knows our every need, cleanse us! Guide us! We cannot repeat it enough! Arrive to deliver us from the pitfalls of this life and help us through all struggles and temptations! O Mary, be sure to be there at the moment of my death!

Contemplation

We know that after death is either Heaven, Hell, or Purgatory. We meditate this day on how painful Purgatory can be, and we search our souls to cleanse habits that might send us there.

Prayer of St. Alphonsus

O Mary, how shall I die? Even now, that I think of my sins, and of that decisive moment on which my salvation or eternal damnation depends, of that moment in which I must expire and be judged, I tremble and am confounded. O my most sweet Mother, my hopes are in the Blood of Jesus Christ and in thy intercession. O comfortress of the afflicted, do not then abandon me, cease not to console me in that moment of great affliction.

(Recitation of the Rosary)

Fourth Day

Our Lady of Guadalupe

Not far from Genazzano, in Rome itself, on Esquiline Hill, had been the miracle of Our Lady of the Snow, where, back in the fourth century, Mary requested a church and indicated where she wanted it by causing snow to fall on the hill one summer morning.

The exact recorded date had been August 5, A.D. 352 and the church that was built, the Basilica of St. Mary Major, was the one where a miraculous Madonna used by Pope Gregory had been kept. If we remember, Gregory had paraded the statue from St. Mary's through the streets of rubble-strewn Rome to rid that chastised city of an epidemic. The madonna was of unstained Oriental wood that, in its dignified countenance and in its majestic demeanor resembled the Virgin of Saragossa. Like the image at Saragossa, it was thought to have supernatural powers.

Upon proceeding through Rome with the image, an apparition of an angel had been seen above a mausoleum near the current-day site of the Vatican, and the plague stopped. It was a statue of Mary with the Christ Child, as she always holds up Jesus, although this time Mary was staring straight ahead, with great power and directness. Make no mistake: this was Mary full of her Son's power. And after he used it in Rome, Pope Gregory sent the image as a gift to the Bishop of Seville in Spain, which was soon under assault by Arab invaders.

As was the case at Montserrat, the statue had to be hidden from the Moslems, who destroyed all Christian images. And again like Montserrat, the faithful chose to hide the statue in a remote cave, this time under a church bell or in an iron casket (accounts differ) in the province of Caceres on the plain of Estremadura near a river known as "Guadalupe," which in the local dialect of this Spanish hinterland meant "hidden channel."

There the statue remained for more than 600 lonely years. Until 1326. That was when Mary appeared in apparition to a humble cowherd named Gil Cordero, who had been searching for a lost cow. Cordero found the cow on a mound of stones, but it was motionless, as if dead. Cordero was ready to cut off its hide when suddenly the cow miraculously sprang up. Cordero was stunned. The animal was alive! But more spectacular still was the apparition of a woman who Cordero spotted coming from the woods.

"Have no fear, for I am the Mother of God, by whom the human race achieved redemption," the woman told Cordero. *"Go to your home and tell the clergy and other people to come to this place where I appear to you and dig here, where they will find a statue."*

This was something the Virgin did across Spain, Italy, and the rest of Europe, appearing at the sites where statues had been lost or hidden and revealing them. Once an image was rediscovered, it was placed in a new chapel, leading to yet hundreds of new churches across Europe.

In this way much of the Church was built. It was one of Mary's chief purposes in the early centuries, and when Cordero did as he was told, telling the local authorities to dig for a statue, he was initially mocked. After all, he was only a simple shepherd with a wild story. But when Cordero insisted on the apparition and showed them the marks on his cow where he was beginning to strip its hide, the noblemen and clerics began to listen. And soon they were proceeding to the site, where they dug at the designated spot and, removing stones and other debris, found the cave and inside it the casket or bell with an ancient document explaining its origin.

It was the image Gregory the Great had sent to Spain in 711. A chapel was built, and it became a huge center of pilgrimage. Thousands arrived from across Spain and other parts of Europe, including Christopher Columbus, who is said to have prayed in front of the image of Guadalupe before setting out across the Atlantic for the New World. Some accounts say he even carried a replica of the wood statue with him!

Mary was ready to cross the great ocean. She was ready to institute her Son's Church in the Americas as she had done in Europe. Anyone who reads about Columbus will quickly learn that he was so devout, especially in his invocation of the Virgin, that he could be described as a Marian mystic. His main ship was named the *Santa Maria* and every evening Columbus and his crew sang the *Hail Mary* as they crossed the Atlantic.

While our secular scholars tell us little of that, Mary was a crucial part of the journey, and when Columbus got to the New World, he and his men named one island "Montserrat" and another "Guadeloupe" (a slightly different spelling). Yet a third was named "El Salvador" for the Savior.

The Virgin was thus at the very foundation of our hemisphere, and the first Christian prayer ever said in our part of the world was the *Salve Regina*, which was also recited by Columbus.

There were many ways Mary was involved with establishment of the New World. America's oldest city, St. Augustine, was founded on the feast of her nativity, and when the Chesapeake Bay was discovered it was originally known as the "Bay of St. Mary."

Indeed, the land surrounding our nation's capital—Virginia and Maryland—can be tied together as "Virgin-Mary-Land." Most astonishing is the fact that French explorers who found the Mississippi River originally called this great waterway not the "Mississippi" but the "River of the Immaculate Conception."

Soon after Columbus arrived in America there was a most astonishing event. It was an event that is connected to the Spanish image of Guadalupe and is our main focus this day. It is one of the major apparitions of all time. It occurred in 1531, in the midst of the Protestant rebellion, the same year Henry VIII took the Church of England away from Rome, and the same year, curiously enough, that the great comet known as Halley's made a major appearance.

The Church in Europe was under assault, but as if to offset the division, Mary appeared on December 9 of that uproarious year to an Aztec convert whom many of you know as Juan Diego. Like the cowherd in Spain, and like so many previous and subsequent seers, Diego was a man of lowly position, at least in the eyes of the world. He lived in a hut with a dirt floor. He was a caring man, a widower who looked after his aging uncle. Juan was about 50 years old, and had been converted to Christianity by the missionaries who came with the Spanish soldiers. In his youth Juan had no doubt been aware of the awesome paganism prevalent in this part of the world, for like the Romans, Greeks, and Egyptians, the Aztecs revered nature spirits, worshipped reptilian idols like the snake, and offered human sacrifices to the various gods and goddesses who seemed like nothing more than evil spirits in disguise.

In fact when Juan was a teenager more than 80,000 were killed in a horrible sacrifice during dedication of the massive temple of Tenochitlan near what is today the sprawling metropolis of Mexico City.

At Tenochitlan they worshipped Quetzalcoatl, the "plumed

serpent," while at a local hill that Juan happened to be walking by on December 9, 1531, they revered a goddess called Tonantzin, the Aztec "mother goddess."

Just as Mary had appeared at Saragossa to dispel paganism, just as she had established Good Counsel to dispel Venus, so too was she now in the New World to begin ridding it of its harmful idols. For as Juan passed the hill, known as Tepeyac, he encountered the sounds of birds singing, which was very strange because it was now winter and most birds did not stay in these parts during the winter months.

When Juan looked up he saw a bright light, climbed to it, and saw a woman in a radiant gold mist, beckoning him and explaining, *"I am the ever-virgin Holy Mary, Mother of the True God. I wish that a temple be erected here without delay."*

Juan was instructed to tell the local bishop of this request just as Cordero was told to summon authorities and just as Mary indicated hundreds of times that she wanted shrines and churches.

But this time it was in the New World, and this series of apparitions was to have monumental effects of Christian conversion. Many of you know the story: Juan went to Bishop Juan de Zumarraga, who was initially very skeptical, as bishops, in their prudence, tend to be. On his way home from the chancery Juan related the disbelief to Mary and she told him to try to convince the bishop again. This Juan did the next day, and seeing the Indian return so soon, the bishop indeed listened with greater interest. But Bishop Zumarraga wanted proof. He wanted a sign from Heaven. Juan related this request to the Virgin and she told him she would provide such a proof the next day.

But there was one hitch: the next day, December 11, Juan's uncle, Juan Bernardino, was desperately ill. The old man had been stricken with *cocolistle*, a contagious and often fatal fever. Juan feared he was dying. He wanted a priest to hear his uncle's last Confession, and so the next day, on December 12, the poor Aztec set about that task instead of going to the top of Tepeyac to visit the Virgin.

As Juan was circumventing the hill, the unexpected happened. Mary descended to intercept him and ask where he was going.

"A servant of yours is very sick," replied Juan. "My uncle. He has contracted the plague, and is near death. I am hurrying to your house (church) to call one of your priests, beloved by Our Lord, to hear his Confession and absolve him, because, since we were born, we came to guard the work of our death. But if I go, I shall return here soon, so I may go to deliver your message. Lady . . . forgive me, be patient with me for the time being. I will not deceive you. . . . Tomorrow I will come in haste."

To this the Most Holy Virgin replied, *"Hear me and understand well, my son the least, that nothing should frighten or grieve you. Let not your heart be disturbed. Do not fear that sickness, nor any other sickness or anguish. Am I not here, who is your Mother? Are you not under my protection? Am I not your health? Are you not happily within my fold? What else do you wish? Do not grieve nor be disturbed by anything. Do not be afflicted by the illness of your uncle, who will not die now of it. Be assured that he is now cured."*

Indeed, at that very same time, the Virgin was appearing to Juan's uncle and healing him. Today there is a sanctuary dedicated to this other apparition at Tulpetlac.

When Juan heard the assurance, he was greatly relieved. The Virgin told him to go to the top of the hill and gather some unusual flowers at the site of her previous apparition. Now remember: this was winter and there were usually no flowers in bloom. Remember too that on such a stony hill, only weeds—thorns and thistles—could be expected.

Yet when Juan Diego got there he was amazed to find many varieties of exquisite roses—*rosas de Castilla*—in bloom! The flowers were extremely fragrant and covered with pearl-like drops of dew. Juan cut them near the petals, placed them in his *tilma* (a burlap-like cloak draped in front of his body), and folded it up to form a large pouch. He then returned to Mary, who asked to see what he had gathered and who rearranged them one by one.

"My son the least, this diversity of roses is the proof and the sign which you will take to the bishop. You will tell him in my name that he will see in them my wish and that he will have to comply to it. You are my ambassador, most worthy of all confidence. Rigorously I command you that only before the presence of the bishop will you unfold your mantle and disclose what you are carrying. You will relate all and well; you will tell that I ordered you to climb to the hilltop, to go and cut flowers; and all that you saw and admired, so you can induce the prelate to give his support, with the aim that a temple be built and erected as I have asked."

In the Aztec language her words were more eloquent. All we have are rough translations. When Juan got back to the chancery, the bishop's assistants, detecting a mysterious and beautiful fragrance around Juan, demanded a look at what he had in his *tilma* and were amazed to see fresh flowers. *But when they tried to take the roses out, the flowers suddenly seemed painted or stamped on Juan's cloth.*

The bishop's men were perplexed, mystified. They took Juan to the prelate's inner office, and that's when Juan knelt before Bishop Zumarraga, unfolded his cloak, and let the roses fall.

The flowers scattered onto the floor, but more amazing was the image Zumarraga saw on the cactus cloak. There on the coarse *tilma* was an exquisitely detailed painting of the Virgin Mary, so very humble-looking, her complexion like wheat, her delicate fingers formed in an aspect of prayer, her nose somewhat slender and long, brows arched and dark, her eyes looking down just as they looked down in the image of Good Counsel, but this time to her right, and this time with no

Child visible.

Instead she was dressed in a sash, which to Aztecs indicated she was with child.

Mary was portrayed in vivid color and unlike a pagan goddess, she wore a cross. Once more, like Good Counsel, there was an expression of gentle concern. She wore a mantle of deep turquoise studded with stars, and there was a *fleur-de-lis* pattern. Her robe was like the robes worn by women in ancient Palestine, and her complexion, as well as the *fleur-de-lis*, reminded scholars of several paintings said to have been done by Saint Luke, including the famous one at Czestochowa!

Most fascinating was the name. The image quickly became known as "Guadalupe," which many believe was because it was immediately connected to the earlier miracle in Guadalupe, Spain, which was well-known not only by Columbus but surely also by subsequent missionaries. "Guadalupe" may have been synonymous with "apparition."

Others say that "Guadalupe" is a phonetic version of the Aztec Nahuatl words for "*coatlaxopeuh*," which is what the Virgin is reported to have said in identifying herself to Juan's uncle. "*Coatlaxopeuh*" is pronounced "quatlasupe" and sounds remarkably like the Spanish word "Guadalupe." "Coa" means serpent, "tla" stands for "the," and "xopeuh" means to crush or stamp out!

Thus Mary had identified herself to Juan's uncle as *coatlaxopeuh*, "the one who crushes the serpent."

It's no wonder the bishop and his men dropped to their knees at first sight of the image. It was a life-sized rendition of Mary, somehow finding its way on a rough agave-cactus cloak. It is like the Shroud of Turin: to this day scientists cannot explain how the image got there. Close inspection by modern researchers have revealed no brushstrokes, no underlying outline, no peeling or fading of the colors, no cracking, no deterioration of the *tilma* (which without preservatives would last but a few decades), no method that could have caused such a delicate image on so rough a surface, no known pigment or paint, and certainly no explanation for why the image, like that of Good Counsel, seems to change when viewed from different positions, its very size and coloration transforming. As one scientist commented, beyond six or seven feet "the skin tone becomes what might best be termed an olive-green, an 'Indian olive,' or gray-green tone. It would seem that somehow the gray and 'caked'-looking white pigment of face and hands combines with the rough surface of unsized *tilma* to 'collect' light, and diffract from afar the olive-skinned hue." The scientist concluded that "such a technique would seem impossible to accomplish by human hands; however, it occurs often in nature. In the coloring of bird feathers and butterfly scales, and on the electra of brightly colored beetles. Such colors are physically diffracted" and "do not depend on absorption and reflection from molecular pigments, but rather on the 'surface-sculpturing' of the feather or the butterfly scales."

There is no bleeding through of paint on the Guadalupe image, nor is there paint between the fibers, nor any flaws. Some of the peripheral images were added later, such as gold rays, a moon, and an angel, but where these show signs of aging, the original image does not.

Perhaps most mysterious is the fact that when scientists studied the image's eyes, they found the corneas are curved precisely like human eyes!

This is shown in the way of several reflections in the eyes, which conform with what would happen in a human one. These mysterious reflections include startling silhouettes. When the Guadalupe eyes are viewed under a microscope, several human figures are reflected in the corneas, one of which seems to be an Indian with his hands lifted in prayer!

Such facts have been detailed for us by scientists like Jody Brant Smith, who says the other figures may include Bishop Zumarraga and his translator, and may be what the image "saw" at the moment the image was revealed on the *tilma*!

It is as if we have a photograph of that momentous event.

We could go on with scientific reasons why this image is miraculous, but I think we need only heed the words of Pope Pius XII, who said the Guadalupe image was "painted with brushes not of this earth." Indeed, it resembles other images that are also of a supernatural origin. So obviously supernatural was Guadalupe that it caused the conversion of eight million Indians in less than ten years. If the Protestants were breaking away from traditional Christianity in Europe, Mary was in the New World rearing an entire new following. And nothing could harm her image. When a bomb went off during the Mexican Revolution in 1921, damaging other objects in the church built at this site, the image was unscathed. Not even its glass encasement broke.

In a time when the unborn are aborted, the pregnant aspect in her image makes her a symbol of the plight of the unborn.

In an era of selfishness, she shows that she favors the humble like Juan Diego.

In an era of uncaring she is there with the most delicate care written across her supernal face.

The image remains to this day at a grand basilica in Mexico City, as striking now as five centuries ago.

Meditation

O Lord God Who sent the Virgin of Guadalupe to us, please let her image remain a beacon to the world and especially a sign to those who would destroy the unborn. O Jesus: please end abortion. Please end euthanasia. Please end illicit birth control. Please end suicide.

Please, O Lord, let us all have life and life more abundantly. Let us all conform ourselves to a style of living that is in conformance with Your creation, with a style of life that is clean and simple and unselfish. Let us focus on the plight of our youngsters, the children who enter a world of such spiritual harassment.

Please, O Lord, let us live a life as humble as that of Juan Diego that like him we may be ever-conscious of death and always prepared for it. O Lord, always let us be prepared. Always remind us of Confession. Always remind us that humility and lowliness are grand in Your sight (even if they are disdained by this blinded world).

Blessed Mother, heal any of our plagues as your original image from St. Mary Major healed plagues and as the shrine in Spain healed pilgrims and as you healed Juan's uncle of *cocolistle*. Heal infectious disease among us and our families.

Heal such disease throughout society, good Lord, and when we are ill, please, O Holy Spirit: please grant us the trust You requested of Juan Diego, that nothing should cause us grief or fear.

Let us pray (response: pray for us)

O Virgin, who gives us prodigies,
O Virgin, who teaches strength,
O Virgin, who takes away fear,
O Virgin, who instills trust,
O Virgin, who watches over our children,
    Pray for us.

Prayer for the sick

Immaculate Mother, Blessed Virgin Mary of Guadalupe, health of the sick, your anointed heavenly hands healed Juan Bernardino and brought us the River of Light, of Life, and of Health: Into your heavenly hands I commend my faith, my hope, and all my sufferings. Please unite them to the Passion of your Son, Jesus Christ, that they may serve as instruments of my salvation and the salvation of all my brothers and sisters. From this moment on, I accept all that the Sacred Heart of your Son may wish to send me. I desire to complete in my life what is lacking to His redeeming Passion. O Blessed Virgin Mary of Guadalupe, I trust that you will give me the strength and all that I need to live with spiritual health and if it serves God's glory and my true well-being, you will give me my physical health also.

Ejaculation

O Mary, so motherly, so kind, heal us and make us whole and let us always be under your glorious turquoise mantle!

Prayer of John Paul II

Virgin of Guadalupe
Mother of the Americas. . .
grant to our homes the grace of loving and
respecting life in its beginnings,
with the same love which you conceived in
your womb the life of the Son of God.
Blessed Virgin Mary, Mother of Fair Love,
protect our families, so that they may always be united,
and bless the upbringing of our children.
We beg you grant us a great love for all the
holy Sacraments, which are, as it were, the
signs that your Son left us on earth.
Thus, Most Holy Mother,
with the peace of God in our conscience,
with our hearts free from evil and hatred,
we will be able to bring to all true joy and
true peace, which come to us from your Son,
Our Lord Jesus Christ, Who with God the Father
and the Holy Spirit, lives and reigns forever
and ever. Amen.

Another prayer from John Paul II

O Immaculate Virgin, mother of the true God and mother of the Church, who from this place reveals your clemency and your pity to all those who ask for your protection, hear the prayer that we address to you with filial trust, and present it to your Son Jesus, our sole Redeemer.

Mother of Mercy, teacher of hidden and silent sacrifice, to you, who comes to meet us sinners, we dedicate on this day all our being and all our love. We also dedicate to you our lives, our work, our joys, our infirmities; for we entrust to your care all that we have and all that we are, our Lady and Mother. We wish to be entirely yours and to walk with you along the way of complete faithfulness to Jesus Christ in His Church. Hold us always with your loving hand.

Virgin of Guadalupe, Mother of the Americas, we pray to you for all the bishops, that they may lead the faithful along paths of intense Christian life, of love and humble service to God and souls. Contemplate this immense harvest, and intercede with the Lord that He may instill a hunger for holiness in the whole people of God, and grant abundant vocations of priests and religious, strong in the faith and zealous dispensers of God's mysteries.

Grant to our homes the grace of loving and respecting life in its beginnings, with the same love with which you conceived in your womb the life of the Son of God. Blessed Virgin, protect our families, so that they may always be united, and bless the upbringing of our children.

Our Hope, look upon us with compassion, teach us to go continually to Jesus and, if we fall, help us to rise again, to return to Him, by means of Confession of our faults and sins in the sacrament of Penance, which gives peace to the soul.

Short prayer

Hail, O Virgin of Guadalupe. We place under your powerful patronage the purity and integrity of the Holy Faith in Mexico and in all the American continent, for we are certain that while you are recognized as Queen and Mother, America and Mexico and our matrimony will be saved. (*one Hail Mary*)

Our Lady of Guadalupe, Mystical Rose, make intercession for the Holy Roman Church, protect the Sovereign Pontiff, help all those who invoke thee in their necessities, and since thou art the ever-virgin Mary, and Mother of the True God, obtain for us from thy most holy Son the grace of keeping our faith, of sweet hope in the midst of the bitterness of life, of burning charity, and the precious gift of final perseverance. Amen. (*one Our Father, Hail Mary, Glory Be in thanksgiving for Guadalupe*)

Morning offering

Immaculate Heart of Mary, heart of my mother, Our Lady of Guadalupe, I unite to thy purity, thy sanctity, thy zeal, and thy love, all my thoughts, words, acts, and sufferings this day, that there may be nothing in me that does not become through thee a pleasure to Jesus, a gain to souls, and an act of reparation for the offenses against thy heart.

Triduum to Our Lady of Guadalupe

"I chose this place and made it holy, in order that my name might be honored, and my eyes and heart might remain there forever" (*2 Chr.* 7:16).

"Who is this that comes forth like the dawn, as beautiful as the moon, as resplendent as the sun . . . ?" (Sng. 6:10)

(*Hail Mary*)

Mary speaks:

"I am the Mother of Fair Love, . . . and of knowledge, and of holy hope . . . My memory is unto everlasting generations" (*Eccl.* 24:24-28, Douay).

O God, You have been pleased to bestow upon us unceasing favors by having placed us under the special protection of the Most Blessed Virgin Mary. Grant us, Your humble servants, who rejoice in honoring her today on earth, the happiness of seeing her face to face in Heaven. Through Christ Our Lord. Amen.

Angelus

V: The angel spoke God's message to Mary
R: And she conceived of the Holy Spirit.
   (*Hail Mary, full of grace. . .*)
V: "I am the lowly servant of the Lord:
R: Let it be done to me according to your word."
   (*Hail Mary. . .*)
V: And the Word became flesh
R: and dwelt amongst us.
   (*Hail Mary. . .*)
V: Pray for us, holy Mother of God,
R: That we may become worthy of the promises of
   Christ.

Let us pray: Lord, fill our hearts with Your grace: once, through the message of an angel, You revealed to us the incarnation of Your Son; now, through His suffering and death, lead us to the glory of His resurrection. We ask this through Christ our Lord. Amen.

Prayer of St. Alphonsus

My most beloved Lady, I thank thee for having delivered me from Hell as many times as I have deserved it by my sins.

Miserable creature that I was, I was once condemned to that prison, and perhaps already, after the first sin, the sentence would have been put into execution, if thou, in thy compassion, hadst not helped me. Thou, without even being asked by me, and only in thy goodness, didst restrain divine Justice; and then, conquering my obduracy, thou didst draw me to have confidence in thee. Ay, my Mother, leave me not in my own hands, for I should then be lost.

Closing prayer

Remember, O most gracious Virgin of Guadalupe, that in your apparitions on Mount Tepeyac you promised to show pity and compassion to all who, loving and trusting you, seek your help and protection.

Accordingly, listen now to our supplications and grant us consolation and relief. We are full of hope that, relying on your help, nothing can trouble or affect us. As you have remained with us through your admirable image, so now obtain for us the graces we need. Amen.

Contemplation

As Mary boldly stood for what was right, and as she leads the struggle for the unborn, so must we do our part in preserving life and the dignity of all humans.

(Recitation of the Rosary)

Fifth Day

Our Lady of the Miraculous Medal

While busy establishing the New World, Our Blessed Mother had not neglected the Old. She appeared to royalty, priests, and even healed an Italian bishop who became Pope Pius II.

Throughout Europe hidden or forgotten shrines continued to be found on hills or in woodlands or in meadows. These were not fairytales. These were not the results of overly devout imaginations. Throughout Europe the Virgin had struggled to contain very real outbreaks of bubonic fever (constantly warning villages that they would suffer unless they repented) and she had revealed yet more miraculous statues hidden in old oaks or obscure caverns.

Germany. England. Austria.

By the 19th century it was in France that the Virgin began to focus her major appearances.

This was to offset the horrible results of the French Revolution.

The Revolution had caused terrible damage to the Roman Church and had led to the deaths of thousands of nuns and priests, not to mention destruction of many famous shrines, but Heaven did not leave Christians alone and once more Christ sent His mother.

Such was best seen in 1830 when the Virgin stepped up her apparitions and began to appear in a more majestic and direct fashion. She now came not just as the gentle matron but as the woman who saves her children by stepping on the head of the serpent. Such was the essence of the famous Miraculous Medal apparitions. The apparitions had started on July 18, 1830, when Our Blessed Mother appeared to St. Catherine Laboure, then a novice, in a beautiful chapel on Rue du Bac in the heart of Paris. Mary had summoned Catherine with an angel late at night and appeared in the convent's chapel. She came as a tangible presence, sitting on a chair at the altar, her clothes audibly rustling. "Looking upon the Blessed Virgin, I flung myself toward her, and falling upon my knees on the altar steps, I rested my hands in her lap," recalled Catherine. "There a moment passed, the sweetest of my life. I could not say what I felt. The Blessed Virgin told me how I must conduct myself with my director, and added several things that I must not tell. As to what I should do in time of trouble, she pointed with her left hand to the foot of the altar, and told me to come there and to open up my heart, assuring me that I would receive all the consolation needed."

Mary explained during the July apparition that there was a special and crucial mission. The Virgin said France and the world were entering evil times but that she would be there to dispense graces.

The following November the Virgin appeared in the way she now is depicted on the Miraculous Medal. She was there with grace flowing from her hands to the entire world. The graces would be for all who asked for them, she said, rich or poor. The luminous rays emanating from her hands spread light downward into a darkening world. On the globe was a green snake with yellow spots that clearly represented evil. "O Mary conceived without sin, pray for us who have recourse to thee," said the front of the medal, while the back had representations of both the Sacred and Immaculate hearts, an "M" interwound with the Cross.

To sit in this unassuming and yet splendid chapel is to feel some of the same graces as when Catherine witnessed the Virgin. Even the chair Mary had sat in is still on the altar. Catherine described her as a woman of unearthly beauty but again it was not superficial beauty. It was the beauty of well-being and goodness. The young nun said Mary was of average height and clothed with white array in a style called "*a la Vierge.*" She wore a high neck and plain sleeves, with a flowing veil that reached the floor. What a ravishing sight! What a graceful beauty! Under the veil her hair was in coils and bound with a fillet ornamented with lace. She came in a style that would appeal to Paris just as she came to places like Guadalupe in a style that would be compatible with those who lived in the Mexican hinterlands.

"Her face was of such beauty that I could not describe it," said Catherine afterwards. "All at once I saw rings on her fingers, three rings to each finger, the largest one near the base of the finger, one of medium size in the middle, the smallest one at the tip. Each ring was set with gems, some more beautiful than others. The larger gems emitted great rays and the smaller gems, smaller rays, the rays bursting from all sides of the base, so that I could no longer see the feet of the Blessed Virgin. At this moment, while I was contemplating her, the Blessed Virgin lowered her eyes and looked at me. I heard a voice speaking these words: '*This globe that you see represents the whole world, especially France, and each person in particular.*' " She showed Catherine an image of the Sacred Heart wrapped in piercing thorns and her own heart punctured by a sword. Then she extended her hands and struck the famous medal pose and an oval-shaped frame formed around her.

Mary had also appeared to Catherine holding a small globe with a Cross on top, praying as she offered it to Jesus, and it was Catherine's distinct impression that the Virgin, in this posture, was praying for the whole world.

When Mary pressed the globe to her chest, an incredible sight ensued: light from diamonds and other precious stones radiated from her maternal hands, showing the beauty of ineffable tenderness.

Here was Mary, still the mother, still so very gentle, but now in direct conflict with Lucifer, whose demons had been unloosed from the pit. She was there to show that she would protect her children. She was there to defeat the devil. It didn't take a loud clash. It didn't always take swords. The devil was clearly paralyzed by her humility and goodness.

If Satan has his legion of fallen angels, we must always remember that Mary comes as Queen of the Heavenly Angels, who are stronger and more numerous.

Wearing the Miraculous Medal grants a special protection against evil. By doing so we are both requesting the protection of Mary and expressing confidence in her. As a result, graces are unleashed. It's crucial to remember this in our own time. I have rarely felt the graces I did while visiting the Paris chapel. It is a reminder that when God wants to move, there is nothing—and no one—who can get in His way. He can cause any miracle He wants to. He can easily erase any evil. Every force in the universe must obey Him. If He chose to—if it was in His plan—God could extinguish all forces of evil with a flick of His finger. He can even make our enemies our friends.

We should remember this as we walk through a world of antagonism. And we should remember the Miraculous Medal as we seek to change our relatives and friends. When we wish to convert someone, there are few better tools than the Miraculous Medal. In 1842, after wearing a Miraculous Medal on a bet, a wealthy Jewish atheist named Alphonse Ratisbonne saw an apparition of Mary and was not only converted but became a Jesuit!

By that time the medal was everywhere. It had become the rage of Christian Europe. Catherine had quietly confided the apparitions to her spiritual director (and no one else, not even her Mother Superior or fellow nuns), and the priest had then taken the medal's design to companies that manufactured the medals by the *millions*. As one bishop noted, except for the Holy Cross, no other Christian symbol was so quickly and widely multiplied. Indeed, in one ten-year period 20 million medals were pressed by one Paris firm alone.

Yet Catherine wanted no glory. She told no one else that she was the seer. And she kept this secret for 46 years, laboring as a lowly laundress for the aged and infirm.

We see here the greatest exhibition of humility, of following Christ's precept that we are to aim our lives only at serving God and fellow humans, and let God take care of everything else. We are not to work for our own pride. We are not to labor in order to impress people. We are not to accumulate material items to keep up with the Joneses. To serve God is to ask God to reveal His Holy Will for our lives—to ask this every day of the week—and to set about each day with eyes only on Him and His plan for the world.

When we work for God, we have peace. We have success. We have security. On the other hand, when we do something for *ourselves*, when we labor for our own gain, such labor loses a great deal of value, no matter how noble or even "religious" our labor may appear on the surface.

If it is our ego we feed—our ego we seek—then we are obscuring the Face of God.

When we are ambitious, when we are competitive, when we use aggressive tactics to achieve an end—and especially when we are jealous—Christ, His mother, and all of Heaven frown upon us.

As Catherine showed so adeptly, a life led with pure intentions, a life led with no seeking of fame, a life led of simple lowliness, elevates the spirit and in the end brings the greatest reward.

If we want peace we need only seek to do God's Will and peace will come.

Catherine Laboure was the symbol of such quiet tranquility. As Father Joseph Dirvin wrote, "It was only in 1876, a scant six months before her death, that the secret greatness of Catherine was finally revealed. Our Lady had asked for the erection of a statue depicting her in the attitude of the first phase of the apparition of November 27, as the 'Virgin of the Globe,' and the statue had not been made. Fearing to appear before Mary Immaculate without every last detail of her mission accomplished, Catherine broke her long silence in order that it might be done."

The statue was indeed molded and the Miraculous Medals continued to spread around the world, numbering today in the hundreds of millions. According to Father Dirvin it is one of only three sacramentals in the history of the Church to be honored with a Mass and an Office, sharing that distinction with the Rosary and Scapular. Special prayers can be said on December 8. But every day we can meditate on Catherine's goodness. She was the "saint of ordinary people" and once more informs us of the power and importance—the crucial importance—of a humble life. Throughout the centuries Mary chose the meek and lowly and humble for her greatest apparitions, the peasants and shepherds on barren hillside as she was once a peasant on the barren and stony hillsides of Nazareth.

What else does this apparition say to us? Just as Catherine's life mission was to serve the infirm and to have the medals struck, so too is there a plan for each of our lives, a plan as important as that given any other person. It may not seem like a grand plan. It may not be flashy. It may not be a public display. But as we have just witnessed with Catherine, God's greatest power is often exhibited in hiddenness. His power resides in humility. His power is in asking God every day of our lives what He wants us to do and pleading with the Holy Spirit to guide us so that we may all accomplish our missions as Catherine finally accomplished hers just months before her death.

Every minute of every day is an opportunity we should not waste to fulfill our own missions.

And so we plead

Dear Christ, You Who so fully completed Your mission, Who did so with such strength, and Who guided St. Catherine to do the same, send the Virgin Mary into our lives to guide us on our own missions. Send the Blessed Mother so that we may make use of every minute that we are on this earth. Send Your mother so that upon death we may be pleasing to You, dear Lord, and have the joy of knowing we accomplished what was assigned to us at birth.

Pray for us, St. Catherine, that we may have our eyes opened to the missions given us by our Creator, and that we may approach life in imitation of your quietness, servitude, and long-suffering. Please, Catherine, help us with a deeper devotion to the Virgin Mary and specifically to the Miraculous Medal. Ask that God grant yet greater graces in our lives as a result of this devotion, and let us too "see" the resplendent lights, the radiant grace, that Jesus gives through the hands of His most holy and Blessed Mother.

O Mary, conceived without sin, wash away our sins and pray for our humility, for our purity, and for the fulfillment of our life work for God the Father! Let us accept what is sent our way and realize God's hidden designs in all challenges and sufferings!

Let us pray (response: pray for us)

O Mary, conceived without sin,
O Mary, streaming grace,
O Mary, who steps on the serpent,
O Mary, who stands on the world,
O Mary, who grants small and great gifts,
O Mary, who helped save France,
O Mary, of the Miraculous Medal,
 Pray for us.

Act of Consecration to Our Lady of the Miraculous Medal

O Virgin Mother of God, Mary Immaculate, we dedicate and consecrate ourselves to thee under the title of Our Lady of the Miraculous Medal. May this medal be for each one of us a sure sign of thy affection for us and a constant reminder of our duties towards thee. Ever while wearing it, may we be blessed by thy loving protection and preserved in the grace of thy Son. O most powerful Virgin, Mother of Our Savior, keep us close to thee every moment of our lives. Obtain for us, thy children, the grace of a happy death; so that, in union with thee, we may enjoy the bliss of Heaven forever. Amen.

Ejaculation

Most Holy Mother exuding Light, be our light always and especially in times of darkness! Teach us to love! Teach us to serve! Teach us to conduct ourselves in a way that touches Heaven!

Angelus

V: The angel spoke God's message to Mary
R: And she conceived of the Holy Spirit.
 (*Hail Mary, full of grace. . .*)

V: "I am the lowly servant of the Lord:

R: Let it be done to me according to your word."

   (*Hail Mary. . .*)

V: And the Word became flesh

R: and dwelt amongst us.

   (*Hail Mary. . .*)

V: Pray for us, holy Mother of God,

R: That we may become worthy of the promises of

   Christ.

Let us pray: Lord, fill our hearts with Your grace: once, through the message of an angel, You revealed to us the incarnation of Your Son; now, through His suffering and death, lead us to the glory of His resurrection. We ask this through Christ our Lord. Amen.

Prayers

Lord Jesus Christ, Who has glorified Your mother, the Blessed Virgin Mary, immaculate from the first moment of her conception, grant that all who devoutly implore her protection on earth may eternally enjoy Your presence in Heaven. Lord Jesus Christ, Who for the accomplishment of Your greatest works have chosen the weak things of the world, that no flesh may glory in Your sight, and Who for a better and more widely diffused belief in the Immaculate Conception of Your mother, have wished that the Miraculous Medal be manifested to St. Catherine Laboure, grant, we ask You, that, filled with humility, we may glorify this mystery by word and work.

Prayer of St. Alphonsus

O Mary, I already know that thou art the most noble, the most sublime, the most pure, the most beautiful, the most benign, the most holy—in a word, the most amiable of all creatures. Pray, pray, and cease not to pray until thou seest me safe in Heaven, beyond the possibility of evermore losing my Lord and certain to love Him forever, together with thee, my dearest Mother.

Novena prayer

Immaculate Virgin Mary, Mother of our Lord Jesus and our Mother, we have confidence in your powerful and never-failing intercession, manifested often through the Miraculous Medal. We your loving and trustful children ask you to obtain for us the graces and favors we ask during this novena if they will be for the glory of God and the salvation of souls. (*Here privately form your petitions.*) You know, O Mary, how often our souls have been the sanctuaries of your Son Who hates iniquity. Obtain for us a deep hatred of sin and a purity of heart which will attach us to God alone so that our every thought, word, and deed may tend to His greater glory. Obtain for us also a spirit of prayer and self-denial that we may recover by penance what we have lost by sin and at length attain to that blessed abode where you are the Queen of Angels and of men. Amen.

O Mary conceived without sin, pray for us: O Mary conceived without sin, pray for us who have recourse to thee.

Additional prayer

O Immaculate Virgin Mary, Mother of Our Lord and our Mother, penetrated with the most lively confidence in your all-powerful and never-failing intercession, manifested so often through the Miraculous Medal, we your loving and trustful children implore you to obtain for us the graces and favors we ask during this novena, if they be beneficial to our immortal souls, and the souls for whom we pray. (*Here form your petition.*) You know, O Mary, how often our souls have been the sanctuaries of your Son who hates iniquity. Obtain for us also a spirit of prayer and self-denial that we may recover by penance what we have lost by sin and at length attain to that blessed abode where you are the Queen of Angels and of men. Amen.

Contemplation

Through the Miraculous Medal even atheists are converted, and so we remember to pray for those who stray, those who sin, those who don't believe, having hope in their conversion instead of judging and condemning them.

(Recitation of the Rosary)

Sixth Day

Our Lady of Lourdes

That Our Blessed Mother was immaculately conceived, that she was born without the taint of original sin, was confirmed during apparitions at the southern end of France in the range of mountains known as the Pyrenees. We can't be sure we know all the details, for the seer, St. Bernadette Soubirous, was an intensely private person. But we do know the main part of her experience occurred between February and July of 1858, when Mary appeared 18 times to her.

This was in a small cave or grotto along the River Gave at the city of Lourdes. Bernadette was out looking for firewood with her sister and a neighborhood friend when the apparitions occurred. She was a humble girl and hailed from a destitute family that was so poor it could not even afford a house but had to find quarters in a donated hovel that once had been the local *cachot* or jail. So cramped were the quarters that for a time Bernadette was sent to live with a family that employed her as a shepherdess.

Most of you know the story but let's meditate a moment on the extraordinary girl, this saint, named Bernadette. At 14 she was an attractive girl with soft, dark, sparkling eyes. She wasn't the best student, but she was a bright girl with an aptitude for sewing, and she was very helpful to her mother, assisting her in the care of the younger children and always willing to run an errand. So lowly and ordinary was Bernadette that no one would have predicted the poor girl would find herself at the center of a momentous supernatural event, apparitions that were to become among the greatest in history, ranking right up there with Guadalupe.

There are several interesting aspects of the Lourdes apparitions that are not widely known. First is the fact that the region had a previous supernatural history. There had been reports of apparitions in the vicinity centuries before Bernadette's own experiences (a mile from the grotto) and we don't know the details but there was also an ancient prediction that one day a great wonder would be wrought in the area. Also intriguing is the fact that, like Catherine, Bernadette was given secrets. Many don't know that secrets were involved at Lourdes but it's true: At least three confidential messages were related to Bernadette, secrets she never revealed, saying they were not even for the Pope.

Bernadette was a very discreet seer, and she never sought to bring attention to herself. This in itself was a sign of authenticity, and so were her ecstasies, which transformed her face in a most beautiful way, eyes intent on the apparition in the grotto, lips moving wordlessly as she prayed the Rosary and communicated with her heavenly visitor. Mary came as a lovely white figure with blue sash and hands clasped in prayer. She was described by Bernadette as wearing the traditional dress of a local religious organization called the Children of Mary, indicating to us once again how she conforms her appearances with the local culture.

"There came out of the interior of the grotto a golden-colored cloud, and soon after a Lady, young and beautiful, exceedingly beautiful, the like of whom I had never seen," explained Bernadette. "She looked at me immediately, smiled at me and signed to me to advance, as if she had been my mother. All fear had left me but I seemed to know no longer where I was. I rubbed my eyes, I shut them, I opened them; but the Lady was still there continuing to smile at me and making me understand that I was not mistaken. Without thinking of what I was doing, I took my rosary in my hands and went on my knees. The Lady made a sign of approval with her head and herself took into her hands a rosary which hung on her right arm. When I attempted to begin the Rosary and tried to lift my hand to my forehead, my arm remained paralyzed, and it was only after the Lady had signed herself that I could do the same. The Lady left me to pray alone; she passed the beads of her rosary between her fingers but she said nothing; only at the end of each decade did she say the *'Gloria'* with me."

This is according to the records kept by a local Lourdes official. A later chronicler of the apparitions, Frances Parkinson Keyes, adds that the Beautiful Lady taught Bernadette a new prayer during the fifth apparition, which the girl continued to recite the rest of her life. Bernadette was also told to bring a blessed candle to the apparition, showing us the potency of this particular sacramental, which was also so important at places like Montserrat. There is an exquisite grace that flows from an anointed candle, bringing a church or home the touch of grace. (If we have a blessed candle we could use it this day during the prayers that follow today's narrative.)

"Pray for sinners," said the Virgin, underlining the serious nature of life and how we must always watch over our own conduct, as well as help other people by praying for their conversion. We are people of God, and when one sinner—just a single sinner—is brought back to the fold, the entire universe is positively affected.

"Penitence," the Virgin had also said, indicating how important it is for all of us to meditate on our faults and atone for them while we're still on earth. *"Penitence, penitence."*

The more we purify ourselves during life—the more we pray and sacrifice is the message—the less time we will spend in Purgatory.

As the Virgin Mary had done at many other apparitions, including ones that were now taking place as far away as South America, she revealed to Bernadette the site for a miraculous spring, and the waters from this well would eventually lead to dramatic and scientifically-documented cures. The Church is extremely careful in accepting any claim of the supernatural, and in the case of healing, it demands the most stringent proof, not only in the way of medical records but in the fact that before an illness can be accepted as proof, it must be an illness that is incurable and could not have gone into remission on its own.

In dozens and hundreds of cases, Lourdes has been able to meet the standard. Paralytics. The blind. Those with severe respiratory disorders or cancer. This causes us to again reflect on the fact that God—the Holy Spirit—can cure anyone He wants to cure. All disease is subject to supernatural intervention. Nothing can defy the Holy Spirit. When God wants us healed, we are cured. Thus, no one is without hope no matter what the circumstances. We already saw this at Saragossa, where a leg was regenerated, and Lourdes has provided many more instances.

God is a healing God, but it must be in accordance with His will. Sometimes God wills that we suffer in order to correct some aspect of our personality or in order for us to spiritually advance. Many times the struggle and sacrifice of ill health are part of God's inscrutable and mysterious plan. Or such tribulation may be needed to purify us. These are things we will not know until the day of reckoning.

We do know that anything physical is subject to the Lord's power, and He has given many powers of healing to the Immaculate Heart of Mary, who heals us of both physical and spiritual darkness. We mention "darkness" because we see in the New Testament how Jesus healed people by first casting out evil spirits. Such spirits can cause many infirmities of mind and body, but they greatly fear the Virgin Mary. She has been granted special power against them. When we have Mary, we have not only the greatest mother but also the strongest of protectors.

The protection places us under that white veil. It was white at Lourdes to emphasize purity. Mary is the ultimate in a holy person. The lesson of sanctity was the one most simply and powerfully conveyed. At Lourdes, Mary is immaculate, and those who follow her are shielded from temptation. Those who follow her are cleansed. It's no idle fact that during the apparitions Bernadette was transformed into radiant beauty. But to enjoy such light we must do our part in detaching from the things of this world. Mary wants detachment. She told Bernadette she could not promise happiness in this world, but only in the next.

"This is the Mother of Angels," said Bernadette. "There can be nothing for me on this earth."

Thus we contemplate the importance of always keeping in mind that earth is a passing place, a temporary place, and while we are here we are on testing ground. We are in exile. This is perhaps the chief message of apparitions through history. God exists and wants us to keep our eyes on the eternal. The Lord is dismayed when we are too focused on the things and creatures of this world. All of life is supposed to be a preparation for Heaven. No matter how successful a person may outwardly seem, if it's material success it cannot lead to true contentment. Earth is not our final destination. And no matter how hard we try, we can never find an earthly utopia. When we are materialistic or lustful, when the physical—the flesh—dictates our lives, we fail miserably.

"Detach, detach, detach" was as much the message from Lourdes as "penitence, penitence, penitence." Indeed in many ways they are the *same* message. For when we get caught up in the things of this world, we need to repent. When we are selfish, we need to confess. When we think chiefly of ourselves we are in need of improvement.

Earthly recognition is nice, but we should never seek it. We should not even want it. God knows the good we do. We do not need to advertise it. While there are times that recognition serves a purpose, that purpose should never be a selfish or aggrandizing purpose. It should never be to feed the ego and make us feel self-important. Those who yearn for prominence in the eyes of men risk losing prominence in the eyes of Christ. Poor are those who need fame, riches, and self-satisfaction.

To shed the material is to take a step toward the kind of beauty exhibited at Lourdes. Indeed, in many ways Lourdes was Mary's most beautiful and delicate appearance. Her wish for a church at this site led to construction of towering and finely chiseled structures, as beautiful as anywhere in the world, and the graces have continued to flow from the grotto, especially the graces of health and well-being. Our Blessed Mother has a special maternal touch at Lourdes.

Lourdes was also an apparition that underscored the importance of discernment. We must always discern what is good and what is not good, whether it be a private matter in everyday life or whether it be the report of a new apparition. There are many reports in our own day, just as there were many back in the days of Lourdes. Although it is not widely known, the fact is that at the same time Bernadette was experiencing her apparitions, others from the vicinity also claimed to see the Virgin. There was a flurry of seers. They came out of the woodwork. Unfortunately, most were false visionaries. All but one of these other alleged seers were rejected by the bishop. There were dozens who seemed self-deceived or deceived by demons that sought to mock, confuse, and dilute the legitimate apparitions seen by Bernadette. There were so many false seers that they nearly caused the entire situation—including Bernadette's apparitions—to be formally condemned!

Fortunately Bernadette's experiences survived, but we thus see the danger of falsity.

Too often the enemy can take the form of an angel of light, deceiving even priests and promoting what seems like the Virgin's cause.

The Church is wise and knows this. It has much experience with mysticism. It must always be obeyed in such discernments, for its officials have been chosen by the Holy Spirit.

Only through the Holy Spirit, only through prayer, fasting, and obedience, and only when we have peace in our hearts can we begin the process of discernment.

More than anything, there is a feeling of cleanliness and love attached to Lourdes, and with love comes grace and healing. Our Blessed Mother invites us to love as she loves, and to become white as she is radiant white. The way of graces was wide open because of Bernadette's pure lowliness. She not only handled everything with humility, but also became, like St. Catherine, a holy nun. And in death her body remains remarkably incorrupt as a sign of the apparition. It can be visited in the city of Nevers.

This is in a nation where traditional Christianity had been attacked as flagrantly as any time since pagan Rome. "Revolutionaries" had destroyed shrines, desecrated chalices, and murdered priests and nuns across this nation, but in the wake of that debacle God had raised up one of the greatest of all shrines and one of the greatest of all nuns.

We clearly see how where evil exists, grace and Heavenly aid also abound.

So does courage. Bernadette had plenty of that also. As would later happen at places like Fatima, she was treated mercilessly by certain local authorities (who threatened to imprison her if she didn't renounce her claims), and her own family doubted her. Yet it was also obvious that Bernadette was not going to back down. She was fervently dedicated to the lady she was seeing, and she was clearly not seeking to be the center of attention, often going to the grotto at times of the day when she hoped no one would notice her. She also had to contend with those who feared the apparition was an evil spirit or a soul from Purgatory. These were legitimate concerns. There are indeed times when purgatorial souls "haunt" us (seeking our prayers), and there are also many deceptions by evil spirits. But the apparitions seen by Bernadette had all the earmarks of heavenly visits, and Mary had clearly come to *banish* the demonic spirit. At one point Bernadette had heard a demonic voice near the river urging her to flee the apparitions and when such noise came another time it was described as a sound like galloping horses, loud and obnoxious. The voice was terrifying but Bernadette raised her arms up to the Blessed Mother and, according to Werfel, Mary's countenance became stern "as though she too had still to wage battles and vanquish her enemies. With wrinkled brow she looked attentively at the river, as though to tame it with her radiant blue eyes. The uproar yielded at once. The hoarse voices crashed into silence. The immemorial rumbling and foaming of the Gave came to the lady's heel like a daunted wolf."

With a simple glance the Virgin dispels our demons.

The very locale of Lourdes may once have been the place of a pagan cult. The caverns in this area had been known for their sacrificial altars. That was why Massabielle, the vicinity of the grotto, was of ill-repute. And that was why the Virgin was coming: once more to purify it, to redeem it as at Tepeyac Hill, to take territory back from the devil.

Do we conduct ourselves likewise? Do we venture onto enemy territory and call down God's blessing? Do we reach out to those who don't know God—who don't know Mary— and attempt to bring them back?

Just as Saragossa emphasized the importance of evangelization, Lourdes had an underlying message of deliverance. We must all work at purging evil. It is the removal of evil that yields the fertility of healing. To fix a wound we must first purge the infection. The Mother of God has been given a special role in this regard. When we call upon her, especially through the Rosary, there is a miraculous feeling of cleanliness. She is a spirit who can heal because she is pure.

And so we pray

O Jesus, Who empowered Your mother to make the momentous appearance at Lourdes, Who gave her the gift of healing, Who sent her as the immaculate woman against the filth of this world, cleanse our own beings and let us know what we need to do and pray to be worthy of similar grace and healing miracles. Especially teach us to properly recite that special gift You have given us through Mary, the Rosary.

Lord Jesus, You are the ultimate physician, You are the One from Whom the Holy Spirit flows. Dear Lord, please look into our bodies and heal any infirmities that afflict us or that may afflict us in the future. Guard us especially against the scourges of cancer and heart disease, which currently take so many lives. Deliver us from genetic disease. Deliver us from disease caused by our food or water or surroundings. By sin or stress. By bacteria. By viruses. Heal our bodies of any hidden or known disorders and do the same, we implore You, great Physician, great Deliverer, for every member of our families and all our friends and acquaintances.

Lord Jesus, at Lourdes there have been countless cures. Sick people bathe in the water and are inexplicably healed, the blind able to see, the lame to walk. Heal us of any major illness we suffer and of any illness that may one day pose a threat, especially any illness that comes due to our sinfulness or the presence of evil spirits. Dear Christ! Chase from our midst all evil! Send Your mother always to quickly expel darkness as she so quickly and easily dispelled evil at the River Gave.

O Mother of Lourdes, O sweet Virgin, O beautiful

Woman, please touch us with your motherly touch and cause balance and healing, health and wholeness, to pervade our physical beings. If it be God's Will let us live long lives serving the Lord, O Blessed Virgin. Let us be here to help others in this place of exile. Grant us longevity to transform this pagan earth.

O Mary, in a new and special way let us feel your sweetness and peace during the Rosary. Come to us as you came to Bernadette. And teach us how to detach from the material things of this world.

Response: pray for us

O Virgin, who was bathed in white at the grotto in
  Lourdes,
O Virgin, who withstood all attempts of the evil one,
O Virgin, who comes to heal,
O Virgin, who raises truth from a sea of falsity,
  Pray for us.

Prayer for specific healing

Virgin Mary, please heal anything that may be wrong in our systems. Sweet Virgin, please heal anything that needs healing in our skeletal systems, in our immune systems, in our circulatory systems, in our brains and nervous systems, in our eyes and ears, in our noses and sinus systems, in our mouths and throats, in our skin and tissue, in our muscles, in our joints, in our hearts, in our lungs, in our stomachs, in the pancreas and thyroid, in our kidneys, in our livers, in our reproductive organs, in our intestines and all other tissues and organs: Heal us, sweet Virgin, through the graces allotted to you by your Son.

Prayer by Abbe H. Perreyve

O Most Holy Virgin, do not—in the midst of thy greatness—forget our earthly sorrows. Cast down thy tender look upon those who suffer, who struggle against difficulties, and who cease not wetting their lips in the bitter draughts of this life. Have pity—I beseech thee—on those who, although united in love, have been cruelly parted, and take pity on the lonely-hearted. Grant us thy help in our unbelief, and have compassion on those most dear to us. Compassionate those who mourn, who pray, who tremble, and grant all hope and peace.

Daily novena

Be blessed, O most pure Virgin, for having vouchsafed to manifest your shining with life, sweetness, and beauty, in the grotto of Lourdes, saying to the child, St. Bernadette, *"I am the Immaculate Conception."* A thousand times we congratulate you upon your Immaculate Conception. And now, O ever Immaculate Virgin, mother of mercy, health of the sick, refuge of sinners, comforter of the afflicted, you know our wants, our troubles, our sufferings. Deign to cast upon us a look of mercy. By appearing in the grotto of Lourdes, you were pleased to make it a privileged sanctuary, whence you dispense your favors, and already many have obtained the cure of their infirmities, both spiritual and physical. We come, therefore, with the most unbound confidence to implore your maternal intercession. Obtain for us, O loving mother, the granting of our request (*here state request*). Through gratitude for your favors we will endeavor to imitate your virtues that we may one day share your glory. Our Lady of Lourdes, mother of Christ, you had influence with your divine Son while upon earth. You have the same influence now in Heaven. Pray for us; obtain for us from your divine Son our special requests if it be the divine Will. Amen.

Ejaculation

O Mary, great and humble queen, heal us in body and spirit!

Lady of Lourdes, you learned from Jesus the love God has for the world. Pray for us, that we may be fully open to that healing love. Amen.

Prayer of St. Alphonsus

O Queen of paradise, who reignest above all choir of angels, and who art the nearest of all creatures to God, I, a miserable sinner, salute thee from the valley of tears, and beseech thee to turn thy compassionate eyes toward me, for whichever side they turn they dispense graces.

Angelus

V: The angel spoke God's message to Mary
R: And she conceived of the Holy Spirit.
  (*Hail Mary, full of grace. . .*)
V: "I am the lowly servant of the Lord:
R: Let it be done to me according to your word."
  (*Hail Mary. . .*)
V: And the Word became flesh
R: and dwelt amongst us.
  (*Hail Mary. . .*)
V: Pray for us, holy Mother of God,
R: That we may become worthy of the promises of Christ.

Let us pray: Lord, fill our hearts with Your grace: once, through the message of an angel, You revealed to us the incarnation of Your Son; now, through His suffering and death, lead us to the glory of His resurrection. We ask this through Christ our Lord. Amen.

Contemplation

Mother, you can go anywhere and the stain of sin touches you not. Let us call upon you at the first hint of pride or lust and keep our every thought charitable and pure!

(Recitation of the Rosary and singing of the song "Immaculate Mary")

Seventh Day

Our Lady of Prompt Succor

Our Blessed Mother's help is not only plentiful, not only generous, but also prompt. She comes when we call. She comes when she hears our pleas. She comes in the way of a mother—hurrying to the side of a child so the child is not further threatened or scared.

It is Mary's special gift to be able to directly respond to our needs in a most timely manner. This has helped build her following. She is immediately involved in our lives and, like a dove, she is always watchful.

Many are those who feel her presence as part of their conversions. Everyone is a child of hers, and she is always ready to assist those who are coming back to the faith. She should thus be invoked in a special fashion for those who have strayed. She can reach into the hardest of hearts. Few can resist the sure and undeniable touch of a mother.

Mary has been allowed to be with us in a very special manner to instill the two vital attributes of salvation: faith and love. We should always meditate upon those virtues and ask ceaselessly that our hearts be filled with tenderness for all people and especially for God. In this way we draw closer to Mary and feel her sure hand with remarkable promptness and power.

In the United States is a remarkable shrine, a truly graced chapel, dedicated precisely to that promptness. She is there under the title of Our Lady of Prompt Succor ("succor" means "aid" or "help"), and the accounts of how quickly she has granted requests—even truly major requests—are legion. "Under this title the Most Blessed Virgin has so often manifested her power and goodness that the religious have unbounded confidence in her," say the chronicles of the nuns who maintain this particular devotion. The chapel is at the Ursuline Convent in the city of New Orleans. It is truly one of the holiest places on the American continent. And the statue itself is the most famous miraculous image in U.S. history (along with a statue of Mary known as *La Conquistadora* in Santa Fe, New Mexico).

Although, compared to Europe, America has very few sites of miracles, this statue ranks with the most ancient and remarkable. It reminds one of the power felt at Montserrat. Again Mary holds the Child, her gown gold, a crown on both her head and that of Jesus, Who holds a small globe with a Cross on top (just like the globe depicted in the Miraculous Medal apparitions). Jesus and Mary are looking in different directions as if each are tending to different but equally pressing matters.

That this statue should have a link to the Miraculous Medal is not surprising in that its history involves France and once again the horrible Revolution. The convent was founded in 1727 and had set about educating the children of European colonists as well as local slaves and Indians. They were the first nuns to arrive in what is now the United States and they founded the oldest school for girls in America. In 1800, when Louisiana was ceded back to France, the good Ursuline sisters were afraid that the horrors of the French Revolution would spread to America. The territory of Louisiana was bouncing between English, French, and American hands, and the nuns, knowing what had happened to their sister nuns in Europe, certainly didn't want to see the French take permanent control. The pope himself, Pius VII, would soon be under arrest in Rome, a captive of Napoleon.

Most of the nuns fled to Havana, Cuba, but seven of the Ursuline sisters remained, and when Louisiana passed into the control of the United States, they anxiously sent President Jefferson a letter asking if their property rights would be honored by the new government. The response from Jefferson is still kept at the convent. "I have received, holy sisters, the letter you have written me wherein you express anxiety for the property vested in your institutions by the former governments of Louisiana," wrote the President. "The principles of the Constitution and government of the United States are a sure guarantee to you that it will be preserved to you sacred and inviolate, and that your institution will be permitted to govern itself according to its own voluntary rules, without interference from the civil authority. . . . Be assured it will meet all the protection which my office can give it."

It was a historic statement but it didn't quite end the Ursulines' worries. There were other problems. They were short staffed. The work was overwhelming. And things got nearly desperate when a mainstay of the community, Mother St. Xavier Farjon, died in 1810. That caused another nun, Sister St. Andre Madier, to appeal to a cousin of hers back in France. The cousin was named Mother St. Michel Gensoul. Sister Andre asked her to come to the U.S. and help the struggling Ursulines.

Mother St. Michel had escaped the deadly wrath of the French Revolution and had much work to do in her own land. France was a mess. Religious communities were under the duress of Napoleon. But Mother St. Michel also realized that the Ursulines in the United States might cease to exist without her help. Inspired by the Holy Spirit, she went to Bishop Fournier of Montpelier and requested leave.

One can imagine the bishop's reaction. He needed Mother St. Michel where she was. He couldn't afford to lose another nun. So many had died during the revolution or fled. "The Pope alone can give this authorization," he told Mother St. Michel. "The Pope alone!"

That was tantamount to refusal, for it was virtually impossible at that time to communicate with the Pope, who was under arrest. Not only was he in the distant city of Rome and not only was mail far less than what it is in our day, but Pius VII had been cut off from the world by Napoleon's men, who held him in custody as they waited to transport him to Fontainebleau. We don't need too much history here. We need only know that the Pope's jailers had received strict instructions not to allow communication. Thus, writing to him was at best a waste of time, an act of folly.

But that didn't stop Mother St. Michel. She knew the Virgin Mary and she knew that if it was God's will, Our Blessed Mother could do anything. With that trust did Mother St. Michel pen a letter to the pontiff on December 15, 1808, setting forth the reason why she wanted to aid her sister nuns in America. "Most Holy Father," she wrote, "I appeal to your apostolic tribunal. I am ready to submit to your decision. Speak. Faith teaches me that you are the voice of the Lord. I await your orders. From your holiness, 'Go' or 'Stay' will be the same to me."

When no opportunity arose for getting the letter out of France, Mother St. Michel prayed before a statue of the Blessed Virgin. "O Most Holy Virgin Mary," she said, "if you obtain a *prompt* and favorable answer to my letter, I promise to have you honored in New Orleans under the title of 'Our Lady of Prompt Succor.' "

Previously Mary had been known as Our Lady of *Perpetual* Succor. There was an ancient and miraculous painting under that title on the island of Crete. Like Our Lady of Good Counsel, this image was moved to Rome during the Turkish invasions. There its great and quick powers were noted when a paralyzed man was immediately healed after the image passed near his home in procession. Countless other miracles were attributed to the image. It was also known as "Our Lady of Never-Failing Help" and "Our Lady of Ever-Enduring Succor." Like the later statue, it shows Mary holding her Child, both crowned, both looking in different directions, the Madonna styled in the Byzantine fashion and gazing at those who looked upon her.

But now there was a new title, a new twist on the ancient name, and a new series of miracles. Soon after her prayer Mother St. Michel's letter finally left Montpelier. The date was March 19, 1809. *And somehow it got to the Pope*, who despite the dire need for nuns in France granted Mother St. Michel's request. Just over a month after the letter was sent—on April 28—Pius had a cardinal send Mother St. Michel a letter saying, "Madame, I am charged by Our Holy Father, Pope Pius VII, to answer in his name. His Holiness cannot do otherwise than approve of the esteem and attachment you have fostered for the religious state. . . . His Holiness approves of your placing yourself at the head of your religious aspirants, to serve as their guide during the long and difficult voyage you are about to undertake."

The prayers had worked and they had been astonishingly prompt. Mother St. Michel ordered a statue carved, and Bishop Fournier, overwhelmed by the miracle, requested the honor of blessing it.

The statue of "Our Lady of Prompt Succor" arrived in Louisiana with Mother St. Michel in 1810.

And nearly immediately there were two momentous miracles.

The first occurred in 1812, when a terrible fire erupted in New Orleans, devastating what we now call the French

Quarter. That was where the convent was at the time (it has since moved to another part of town). The fire was a true holocaust and, propelled by the wind, was heading right for the Ursuline convent.

That was when one of the nuns placed a small statue of the Virgin on a window facing the fire and Mother St. Michel again began to implore the Virgin. "Our Lady of Prompt Succor, we are lost unless you hasten to our aid!"

It is said that the wind instantly shifted, driving the fire away.

The Ursuline convent was one of the few buildings spared destruction!

Such events show us that nothing is beyond the reach of prayer, no problem, no disaster. Three years after the hellish fire, in 1815, yet more trouble haunted New Orleans during the war between the Americans and British. By this time Louisiana was a part of the United States, but England was looking to confiscate the former territory. The British arrived near New Orleans on the plains of Chalmette to square off against Andrew Jackson, the famous American general.

This too was an amazing and well-documented miracle. For there was no way the Americans could win. The British had 15,000 troops. The American force was 6,000. It looked like the Americans—and the city of New Orleans—were doomed.

The night of January 7 the Ursuline sisters went before the Blessed Sacrament and stayed there through the night. Others joined them in the chapel, praying and weeping before the holy statue. On the morning of January 8 the vicar general offered Mass at the main altar, above which the statue had been placed. The prayers were said in special earnest, for the thundering of cannons had been heard by all in the chapel.

At Communion time—at the very moment of the Eucharist—a courier rushed into the chapel to inform all present that the British had been miraculously defeated. They had been confused by a fog and had wandered into a swamp, in full view of the waiting Americans, who fired upon them from unseen positions.

About 2,600 British were lost while the Americans suffered very few casualties.

It was not Our Blessed Mother who killed the British. It was not Mary who initiated battle. But it was the Blessed Virgin who came to the aid of the just who implored her.

"The result seems almost miraculous," admitted a local newspaper, the *Picayune*. "It was a remarkable victory, and it can never fail to hold an illustrious place in our national history."

General Jackson himself went to the convent to thank the nuns for their prayers. "By the blessing of Heaven, directing the valor of the troops under my command, one of the most brilliant victories in the annals of war was obtained," he proclaimed to his troops, describing the victory in a letter to the vicar as a "signal interposition of Heaven."

Rome has officially approved devotion to Our Lady of Prompt Succor and the statue was solemnly crowned through a decree issued by Pope Leo XIII. A Mass of thanksgiving is celebrated on January 8.

The old convent remains the oldest building in the Mississippi valley but no longer houses the statue or convent, which are now located on State Street. But the feeling around the statue is still tangible. The graces still flow. Many favors are still granted. We see in this case the powerful and fast way the Virgin can operate when pious people come to her in faith. We see also the same lesson as from Saragossa, that the graces are associated with her Son. The great 1815 victory came after a night in front of the Blessed Sacrament and then was announced during holy Communion, leaving us no doubt as to the source—the wellspring—of Mary's miracles.

In our own lives we have many needs we would like to see met as soon as possible, urgent worries, compelling concerns.

When we want a quick answer, when we want a quick favor, even in an "impossible" situation, this is a devotion that will accomplish such requests if they are the will of the Father.

And so we pray

Lord Jesus, we know You are the ultimate power. We know that when You grant graces through Your mother they can come to us faster than the speed of light, with unfathomable power. Dear Lord, let us grow closer to You through Our Lady of Prompt Succor, that we may please God and that He may come to our assistance in a hasty fashion.

Grant us the faith, that we too may see miracles in our lives, and grant us the inspiration and grace to pray fervently during Mass and at the Blessed Sacrament.

And O Mary, you have come so many times through history to aid your children. Come now to our aid. Come to the prompt aid of our families. Come to the aid of the United States, which has sunken into materialism and unholiness and darkness.

Save us, Blessed Mother. Save our nation. Save the heritage that men like General Jackson fought for. Save this great country founded upon the precepts of Christianity. Bring back holiness, O Lord. Bring back goodness. Rescue our nation as quickly as possible!

In our own lives, instill a fervent faith and love. O Blessed Mother, let us feel love for all human beings. Let our hearts soften. Let us become your vessels of purity and charity.

Response: be with us

O Virgin so gracious,
O Virgin, who saved France,
O Virgin, who beckons New Orleans,
O Virgin, who can save our own nation,

O Virgin of quick response,
O Virgin, who instills charity,
   Be with us.

Ejaculation

Virgin Mary of Prompt Succor, be ever and quickly attendant to our needs!

Angelus

V: The angel spoke God's message to Mary
R: And she conceived of the Holy Spirit.
   (*Hail Mary, full of grace. . .*)
V: "I am the lowly servant of the Lord:
R: Let it be done to me according to your word."
   (*Hail Mary. . .*)
V: And the Word became flesh
R: and dwelt amongst us.
   (*Hail Mary. . .*)
V: Pray for us, holy Mother of God,
R: That we may become worthy of the promises of
   Christ.

***Let us pray*:** Lord, fill our hearts with Your grace: once, through the message of an angel, You revealed to us the incarnation of Your Son; now, through His suffering and death, lead us to the glory of His resurrection. We ask this through Christ our Lord. Amen.

Let us further pray (longer and optional prayers but ones that bring grace)

Our Lady of Prompt Succor, you are after Jesus our only hope. O Most Holy Virgin, whose merits have raised you high above angel choirs to the very throne of the Eternal and whose foot crushed the head of the infernal serpent, you are strong against the enemies of our salvation. O Mother of God, you are our mediatrix most kind and loving. Hasten, then, to our help, and as you did once save your beloved city from ravaging flames and our country from an alien foe, do now have pity on our misery, and obtain for us the graces we beg of you. Deliver us from the wiles of Satan, assist us in the many trials which beset our path in this valley of tears, and be to us truly Our Lady of Prompt Succor now and especially at the hour of our death. Our Lady of Prompt Succor, O Mary Immaculate, you are the model of all virtues, the path by which we go to Jesus, the mysterious channel through which divine favors are imparted to us. You have such power over the Heart of Jesus, hasten to our assistance and obtain our earnest request (*here name the favor desired*).

In you, O Mary, we put our trust. Let it not be said that our hopes have been frustrated. O Mother most chaste, be our strength against temptation, our help in danger, our consolation in sorrow, but especially Our Lady of Prompt Succor at the hour of our death. Amen.

Our Lady of Prompt Succor, hasten to help us. (Repeat three times and recite the *Hail Mary* and *Our Father*.)

Litany of Our Lady of Prompt Succor

Lord, have mercy on us.
Christ, have mercy on us.
Lord, have mercy on us.
Christ, hear us.
Christ, graciously hear us.
God the Father of Heaven, have mercy on us.
God the Son, Redeemer of the world, have mercy on us.
Holy Trinity, one God, have mercy on us.
Holy Mary, pray for us.

Mother of the Infant Jesus, pray for us.

Our Lady of Prompt Succor, pray for us.

Our Lady of Prompt Succor of all who invoke you
with confidence, pray for us.

Our Lady of Prompt Succor of all who are devout
toward the Infant Jesus, pray for us.

Our Lady of Prompt Succor for obtaining a lively faith,
pray for us.

Our Lady of Prompt Succor for sustaining the hope of
Christians, pray for us.

Our Lady of Prompt Succor for obtaining and
persevering in charity, pray for us.

Our Lady of Prompt Succor for observing the law of
God, pray for us.

Our Lady of Prompt Succor for observing perseverance in
virtue and good works, pray for us.

Our Lady of Prompt Succor in every spiritual necessity,
pray for us.

Our Lady of Prompt Succor against the revolt of self-
will, pray for us.

Our Lady of Prompt Succor in the occasion of sin, pray
for us.

Our Lady of Prompt Succor in every temptation, pray
for us.

Our Lady of Prompt Succor against the evil spirit, pray
for us.

Our Lady of Prompt Succor for obtaining contrition,
pray for us.

Our Lady of Prompt Succor of those wishing to re-enter
the path of salvation, pray for us.

Our Lady of Prompt Succor for the conversion of sinners,
pray for us.

Our Lady of Prompt Succor in every temporal
necessity, pray for us.

Our Lady of Prompt Succor in every affliction, pray for us.

Our Lady of Prompt Succor of afflicted families, pray for us.

Our Lady of Prompt Succor of the sick and the poor, pray for us.

Our Lady of Prompt Succor against contagious diseases and epidemics, pray for us.

Our Lady of Prompt Succor in every accident, pray for us.

Our Lady of Prompt Succor against destruction by fire, pray for us.

Our Lady of Prompt Succor against lightning and tempest, pray for us.

Our Lady of Prompt Succor against destruction by flood, pray for us.

Our Lady of Prompt Succor of travelers, pray for us.

Our Lady of Prompt Succor of navigators, pray for us.

Our Lady of Prompt Succor of the shipwrecked, pray for us.

Our Lady of Prompt Succor against the enemies of our country, pray for us.

Our Lady of Prompt Succor in time of war, pray for us.

Our Lady of Prompt Succor of those aspiring to the holy priesthood and the religious life, pray for us.

Our Lady of Prompt Succor of laborers in the Lord's vineyard, pray for us.

Our Lady of Prompt Succor of missionaries who spread the faith, pray for us.

Our Lady of Prompt Succor of our Holy Father the Pope, pray for us.

Our Lady of Prompt Succor for those searching for the faith, pray for us.

Our Lady of Prompt Succor against the enemies of the Church, pray for us.

Our Lady of Prompt Succor at the hour of death, pray
for us.
Our Lady of Prompt Succor for the deliverance of the
souls in Purgatory, pray for us.

Lamb of God, Who takes away the sins of the world,
spare us, O Lord.
Lamb of God, Who takes away the sins of the world,
graciously hear us, O Lord.
Lamb of God, Who takes away the sins of the world,
have mercy on us.

Our Lady of Prompt Succor, pray for us.
That we may be made worthy of the promises of
Christ.

O Almighty and Eternal God, Who sees us surrounded by
so many dangers and miseries, grant in Your infinite goodness
that the Blessed Virgin Mary, Mother of Your Divine Son, may
defend us from the evil spirit and protect us against all
adversities, that always and with prompt succor she may
deliver us from every evil of soul and body, and safely guide us
to the kingdom of Heaven, through the merits of Our Lord
Jesus Christ, Your Son, Who lives and reigns with You in the
unity of the Holy Spirit, One God, world without end. Amen.

Contemplation

If our eyes are always on Heaven and God, at the end of
life we will find ourselves in His Presence.

(Recitation of the Rosary)

Final Prayers

Lord, have mercy. Christ, have mercy. Lord, have mercy. Christ, hear us. Christ, graciously hear us. God the Father of Heaven, have mercy on us. God the Son, Redeemer of the world, have mercy on us. God, the Holy Spirit, have mercy on us. Holy Trinity, One God, have mercy on us.

Litany of Loreto (*response: pray for us*)

Holy Mary,
Holy Mother of God,
Holy Virgin of virgins,
Mother of Christ,
Mother of divine grace,
Mother most pure,
Mother most chaste,
Mother inviolate,
Mother undefiled,
Mother most amiable,
Mother most admirable,
Mother of good counsel,
Mother of our Creator,
Mother of our Savior,
Virgin most prudent,

Virgin most venerable,
Virgin most renowned,
Virgin most powerful,
Virgin most merciful,
Virgin most faithful,
Mirror of justice,
Seat of wisdom,
Cause of our joy,
Spiritual vessel,
Vessel of honor,
Singular vessel of devotion,
Mystical rose,
Tower of David,
Tower of ivory,
House of gold,
Ark of the Covenant,
Gate of Heaven,
Morning star,
Health of the sick,
Refuge of sinners,
Comforter of the afflicted,
Help of Christians,
Queen of Angels,
Queen of Patriarchs,
Queen of Prophets,
Queen of Apostles,
Queen of Martyrs,
Queen of Confessors,
Queen of Virgins,
Queen of all Saints,
Queen conceived without original sin,
Queen assumed into Heaven,
Queen of the most holy Rosary,
Queen of peace,
   Pray for us.

Litany of some approved apparitions
(response: pray for us)

Mary, seer of Gabriel,
Mary, guide of the Light,
Mary, destined to be great,
Mary, who helps to redeem,
Mary, crowned in Heaven,
Mary, entrusted by our Lord,
Mary of Saragossa,
Mary of Le Puy,
Mary of Montserrat,
Mary of Mount Carmel,
Mary of Knock,
Mary of Lourdes,
Mary of Pontmain,
Mary of Prouille,
Mary of Vladimir,
Mary of Pochaiv,
Mary of Constantinople,
Mary of Kiev,
Mary of Hrushiw,
Mary of Fatima,
Mary of Mary Major,
Mary of Genazzano,
Mary of La Salette,
Mary of Estredamura,
Mary of Guadalupe,
Mary of New Orleans,
Mary of Evesham,
Mary of Lujan,
Mary of Rue du Bac,
Mary of Vinay,
Mary of Le Laus,
Mary of Chartres,

Mary of the Catacombs,
Mary of Syracuse,
Mary of Cap-De-La-Madeleine,
Mary of Clairefountaine,
Mary of Walsingham,
Mary of Covadonga,
Mary of Rocamadour,
Mary of the Philippines,
Mary of the Cape,
Mary of Jasna Gora,
Mary of Frascati,
Mary of Loreto,
Mary of Banneux,
Mary of Beauraing,
Mary of Rome,
Mary of Nazareth,
Mary of all authentic apparitions . . .
    Pray for us.

Lamb of God Who takest away the sins of the world,
    spare us, O Lord!
Lamb of God Who takest away the sins of the world,
    graciously hear us, O Lord!
Lamb of God Who takest away the sins of the world,
    have mercy on us.

Pray for us, O holy Mother of God, that we may be
    worthy of the promises of Christ.

Notes

First Day: For Ephesus see *Ephesus, Legends and Facts* by Dr. Cemil Toksoz (Ayyildiz Matbaasi, 1962). For images reputedly painted by Luke, see *The Madonna of St. Luke* by Henrietta Irving Bolton (G.P. Putnam's Sons, 1895). For Spain see *A Concise History of Spain* by Henry Kamen (Charles Scribner's Sons). For Saragossa see page 4 of *The Irish Catholic* (an article by John E. Keller on November 7, 1968); *Apparitions and Shrines of Heaven's Bright Queen* by William Thomas Walsh (Burns & Oates, 1904); *Shrines to Our Lady Around the World* by Zsolt Aradi (Farrar, Strauss, and Young, 1954); *Historic Shrines of Spain* by Isabel Allardyce (Franciscan Missionary Press, 1912); *All Zaragoza* (Editorial Escudo de Oro, S.A., a guidebook sold at the site); *The Last Secret* by Michael H. Brown (Servant Publications, 1998); and *Butler's Lives of the Saints*, edited and supplemented by Herbert J. Thurston, S.J. and Donald Atwater (Christian Classic, 1956). Also, I investigated this site in person. The generational prayer came off the internet and was said to be a Marianist prayer by a priest named Rev. Joseph H. Lackner, S.M. The prayers from St. Alphonsus come from his book *The Glories of Mary* (Redemptorist Fathers, 1931).

Second Day: For Czestochowa see *Miraculous Images of Our Lady* by Joan Carroll Cruz (Tan Books, 1993) and "Theology of a Marian Shrine" by Marian Zalecki, O.S.P., Marian Library Studies, volume 8 (University of Dayton, 1976). For Montserrat see *The Montserrat* by Jose Maria de Sagarra (Editorial Noguer, Barcelona, 1956); *All Montserrat* (Editorial Escudo de Oro, S.A., available at Montserrat); *Historic Shrines of Spain* (cited above); and *Miraculous Images of Our Lady* (cited above). Also, I personally visited Montserrat. The Consecration to Jesus is an excerpt from a consecration in "Preparation for Total Consecration according to Saint Louis Marie de Montfort" (Montfort Publications).

Third Day: Much of the background on Good Counsel comes from the seminal work, *The Virgin Mother of Good Counsel* by Monsignor George F. Dillon D.D. (Benziger Brothers, 1886). See also *The Virgin Mother of Good Counsel* by E.A. Selley (Cashman, Keating & Co., 1889) and also *Miraculous Images of Our Lady* as cited above.

Fourth Day: My main source here was an ancient document called "the Nican Mopohua," which was the earliest known record, written originally by Antonio Valeriano in the 16th century. It is to be found, along with much else I relied upon, in Jody Brant Smith's excellent book, *The Image of Guadalupe*, the most interesting book on Guadalupe I have seen (Mercer University Press, 1994). It is from page 64 of this book that I took the quote from the scientist. See also *A Woman Clothed with the Sun* edited by John J. Delaney (Image Books, 1961). Also, I personally visited Guadalupe.

Fifth Day: For the Miraculous Medal there are many sources, including *A Woman Clothed With the Sun* (cited above); "The Saint of Silence and the Message of Our Lady," a pamphlet issued at the site; another pamphlet called "Our Lady of the Miraculous Medal" by the Daughters of St. Paul in Boston; *Blessed Catherine Laboure* translated from the French, Edmond Crapez (St. Joseph's, 1933); *The Sun Her Mantle* by John Beevers (Newman Press, 1953); and prayers from the Association of the Miraculous Medal in Perryville, Missouri (800-264-MARY), which also provides some of the prayers in novena booklets. Also I personally visited this site and collected literature there.

Sixth Day: My main sources for Lourdes, in addition to two personal visits there, were *The Song of Bernadette* by Franz Werfel (The Viking Press, 1942); *A Woman Clothed with the Sun* (previously cited, and the source for the long quote from the local authority); and *Encountering Mary* by Sandra L. Zimdars-Swartz (Princeton University Press, 1991). As in other cases, certain prayers have been taken off the internet, where they appear without copyright.

Seventh Day: I researched Our Lady of Prompt Succor by personally visiting this grace-filled chapel, and I relied upon a manual of devotions given there and available by writing the National Shrine of Our Lady of Prompt Succor, 2635 State Street, New Orleans, Louisiana, 70118. I also relied upon: *Cause of Our Joy* by Sister Mary Francis LeBlanc (St. Paul Editions, 1976); *Miraculous Images of Our Lady* (cited above); *Apparitions of Heaven's Bright Queen* (also referenced above); and *A Century of Pioneering* by Sister Jane Frances Heaney (published by the Ursuline Sisters in 1993). I urge pilgrimages to the chapel of Our Lady of Prompt Succor, where graces flow like some of the famous shrines in Europe and where we need to intercede for beleaguered America.

OTHER BOOKS BY MICHAEL H. BROWN

The Final Hour

Akita, Betania, Fatima, Garabandal, Knock—all obscure places on the maps. Or are they? Has the Mother of Jesus appeared at these and other international locations? Why?

1-880033-03-8   368 pages, color photos

After Life
What it's like in Heaven, Hell, and Purgatory

What happens when we die? How are we judged? How do we prepare? These are some of the questions addressed in this book. Catholic and scientific literature, as well as interviews with those who have had brushes with death, provide glimpses of the afterlife.

1-880033-25-9   120 pages

The Trumpet of Gabriel

Michael H. Brown explores today's fascination with angels and other spiritual or supernatural phenomena. People from many walks of life—as well as many religious denominations—believe these are God's call for mankind to reform.

1-880033-16-X   320 pages

Secrets of the Eucharist

The continuous True Presence of Christ with us in the Blessed Sacrament is good news worth sharing! This book of heart-felt reflections on the Holy Eucharist demonstrates that devotion to this profound Sacrament is fundamental to our Faith.

1-880033-23-2   96 pages

Witness—Josyp Terelya
An autobiography, co-authored by Michael H. Brown

The amazing story of a dynamic, contemporary mystic, suffering servant, and victim of communism—having been imprisoned for years in Soviet gulags—*Witness,* published before the collapse of the Soviet Union, is a story of supernatural events and accurate predictions.

1-877678-17-1   344 pages, color photos

Prayer of the Warrior

Spiritual warfare is at an all-time high. Many testimonies from those in the "front lines" of the combat have been received, indicating the timeliness and importance of this book. It provides unique insight into the battle now raging between good and evil.

1-880033-10-0   256 pages